DRAMÉTIS

Three Métis Plays

DRAMÉTIS

Three Métis Plays

Greg Daniels
Marie Clements
Margo Kane

Theytus Books Ltd.
Penticton, BC

Canada Cataloguing in Publication Data

Main entry under title:

DraMétis

ISBN 0-919441-94-7

1. Canadian drama (English)--Métis authors. * 2. Canadian drama (English)--21st century. * I. Daniels, Greg, 1959- II. Clements, Marie Humber, 1962- III. Kane Margo.
PS8307.D72 2001   C812'.608'0897   C2001-911500-8
PR9196.37.I5D72 2001

Editorial: GregYoung-Ing, Leanne Flett Kruger
Layout: Leanne Flett Kruger, Florene Belmore
Cover Design: Julie Flett
Proofing: Leanne Flett Kruger, Chick Gabriel
Cover Photo: Greg Young-Ing (photo of Margo Kane)

Theytus Books Ltd.
Lot 45, Green Mountain Rd.
RR 22, Site 50, Comp 8.
Penticton, BC
V2A 6J7

The publisher acknowledges the support of The Canada Council for the Arts, The Department of Canadian Heritage, The British Columbia Arts Council and The Saskatchewan Arts Board in the publication of this book.

CONTENTS

Theytus Books is proud to publish this anthology which will make a valuable contribution to the growing discipline of Métis drama. The works included herein represent important authors and/or works whose publication are long overdue, including: *Percy's Edge* by Greg Daniels, *Age of Iron* by Marie Clements and Margo Kane's work in progress, *Confessions of an Indian Cowboy.*

Greg Daniels'*Percy's Edge* was produced at the 25th Street Theatre in Saskatoon in May, 1995. This was Daniels' third play to be produced and is considered to be his most epic work, which established him as a senior playwright in the world of Métis drama. Although the play is relatively long, the cast, set and production is minimalist; yet it portrays a powerful story of interdependent and conflicting relationships among socially marginalized characters who struggle to survive and find meaning in their lives.

Age of Iron is the first play written by the renowned playwright/ actor, Marie Clements. It was produced at Vancouver's historic Firehall Arts Centre in October, 1994. Clements' first production, this innovative work brought to stage was a clear indication that she would push the envelope of contemporary theatre, a career path which she has since continued to forge.

Confessions of an Indian Cowboy, written and performed by Margo Kane, was first produced as a work-in-progress at the Main Dance studios in Vancouver, June 2000. Immediately following there was a run-out performance at the En'owkin Centre in Penticton for Coyote's Roundup, a National Aboriginal Theatre Conference on June 24, 2000. More development produced another draft which was performed at Millenium Place in Whistler, BC, June 2001. *Confessions of an Indian Cowboy* is poised to be regarded alongside Kane's *Moonlodge* as another landmark solo work in Métis, Aboriginal and Canadian theatre.

PERCY'S EDGE

by

Greg Daniels

CAST OF CHARACTERS

PERCY: Native man, 50. Victor's father.
VICTOR: Native man, 32. Percy's son.
FAITH: Native woman, 20. Victor's girlfriend.
MARK: Non-Native man, 31. Victor's friend.
MOSES: A turtle. Percy's friend.

ACT I.

Evening. Victor, Faith and Mark on the street. Mark drinks from a whiskey bottle. Victor is at Faith's feet, applying green nail polish.

VICTOR:

How am I doing?

FAITH:

It's okay.

VICTOR:

Yeah?

FAITH:

Yeah.

VICTOR:

You're sure now?

FAITH:

Looks good to me.

VICTOR:

That's good. Right on. (*slight pause*) You tell me if I'm fucking it up, okay?

FAITH:

I will.

VICTOR:

Make sure. (*slight pause – to himself*) Man, do I do good work or what? Too deadly. Way too fucking deadly. (*to Faith*) Know what I mean?

FAITH:

You're good?

VICTOR:

That's exactly right, little girl.

MARK:

Vic. (*drinks*) Vic.

VICTOR:

What?

MARK:

You busy?

VICTOR:

No, I'm kneeling for nothing, pal. What do you think?

MARK:

Never mind. It'll keep.

VICTOR:

(*to Faith*) Keep still. (*pause – to Mark*) What the hell you talking about, it'll keep? You have something to say, say it. Don't be pulling my fucking chain like that. Talk to me. Talk to me for fuck sake.

MARK:

Later.

VICTOR:

Suit yourself. (*to Faith*) Thought I told you to keep still. (*slaps her foot*)

FAITH:

Don't, that hurts.

VICTOR:

(*sarcastically*) Don't, that hurts. Little love tap like that don't hurt.

FAITH:

Of course it does.

VICTOR:

No, it doesn't. That was nothing.

FAITH:

I don't like being hit. I bruise easy. Just a little bump and I get a bruise. (*examining her foot*) It's already turning blue. Don't do that again.

VICTOR:

Good thing about a bruise is that it always goes away. (*slight pause*) I don't know about you, little girl. What you need is some good old-fashioned Indian love. Toughen you up.

FAITH:

That's sick.

VICTOR:

Thank you. Give me your foot. So what's on your mind there, Mark?

MARK:

Nothing.

VICTOR:

Nothing? Bullshit. (*to Faith*) You're moving again.

MARK:

Forget it, Vic, it's gone.

VICTOR:

Yeah, well, fuck ya then.

MARK:

Jesus.

VICTOR:

What?

MARK:

When are you gonna learn some new words?

VICTOR:

What do you mean?

MARK:

It's the way you talk, Vic.

VICTOR:

What's wrong with the way I talk?

MARK:

Everything with you is fuck. Fuck me. Fuck you. Fuck off. Fuck this, that and the other thing. Gets hard on the ears, Vic, you know?

VICTOR:

Really?

MARK:

Yeah.

VICTOR:

Well, fuck ya then. (*laughs*) Left yourself wide open for that one.

MARK:

Yeah. That was a good. Here, have a drink, Vic.

VICTOR:

Get that alcoholic shit away from me or I'll tear your arm off.

MARK:

Don't do that. I need my arm. Tearing arms off is bad, Vic.

VICTOR:

Well, don't fuck around then or you'll lose it. (*to Faith*) What do you think? You think I swear too much?

FAITH:

Maybe a little.

VICTOR:

No shit? (*slight pause, to the two*) Actually, I really, really don't give a flying fuck about the way I talk. You don't like it, stick your fingers in your fucking ear holes or look at a cloud or something.

MARK:

Harsh, Vic. That's harsh, man. Harsh. Harsh.

FAITH:

I need to move.

VICTOR:

I dare you.

FAITH:

My back is sore.

MARK:

She needs to move, Vic. Let her move. Her back is sore. Have a heart, man.

VICTOR:

You ever hear the expression mind your own fucking business?

MARK:

Yeah. Why?

VICTOR:

Well do it, that's why. (*slight pause*) She don't need my permission to move. She can move or not move any time she feels like it. (*to Faith*) Go ahead, move if you want. Matter of fact, lay down.

FAITH:

What?

VICTOR:

Lay down.

FAITH:

Here?

VICTOR:

Why not?

FAITH:

It's hard.

VICTOR:

So? Lay back. Relax… Close your eyes and let Dr. Vic do his work.

FAITH:

You crazy?

VICTOR:

Yeah. So be a good little girl and lay down for daddy.

FAITH:

What if the police come?

VICTOR:

What if the police come? Fuck them. What can they do? We ain't doing nothing wrong. What are they gonna do? They gonna bust me for painting your toes? I doubt it very much.

MARK:

(*drinks*) I don't know, Vic. They can bust you for any damn thing they want. Including painting your old lady's toes. Cause like, you know, they have the power… (*drinks*) to do that.

VICTOR:

Fuck that. If it wasn't for their guns and badges and sticks and striped pants and two-way fucking radios, they wouldn't have no fucking power. Fuck them and their power.

MARK:

Okay.

VICTOR:

(*to Faith*) So lay down. (*pause*) You do the rest. (*hands her the nail polish and some spills on her shoe*) Whoa, fuck me blind. That was an accident.

FAITH:

I know.

VICTOR:

Good. Long as you know. Sorry about that.

MARK:

(*to Faith*) Use these. (*takes some napkins from his back pocket*) Might come off.

VICTOR:

I'll do it. (*takes the napkins*)

FAITH:

Don't smear it.

VICTOR:

(*with the shoe*) I won't smear nothing.

MARK:

I don't know, Vic, you don't want to smear it. I think maybe the best thing to do is let it dry, then peel it off.

VICTOR:

That's where you're wrong. You let it dry, you're gonna leave a stain. Get it while it's fresh and you'd never know it was there.

FAITH:

I'll do it.

VICTOR:

No, no. Just hang tough. I'll take care of it. (*wipes the shoe*) Smeared a bit. Not as bad as I thought it would. It'll have to do.

FAITH:

That's the only shoes I have.

VICTOR:

Don't worry about it. The world is fulla shoes, little girl.

FAITH:

Let me see.

He gives her the shoe and the napkin.

VICTOR:

That's not so bad. I seen worse. Why don't you take them inside and run a little cold water on them.

FAITH:

Where?

VICTOR:

Inside. Up the stairs to your left, there's a washroom there. Anyone bothers you, tell 'em to fuck off. Can you do that?

FAITH:

Who's up there?

VICTOR:

I don't know. Might be someone there.

FAITH:

What about my feet?

VICTOR:

What about them?

FAITH:

They're not done.

VICTOR:

So?

FAITH:

Doesn't look right. One foot is done and the other one isn't.

VICTOR:

That's okay. I'll finish when you get back.

FAITH:

You'll wait for me?

VICTOR:

I'm not leaving. I'll be here.

MARK:

We're not going anywhere.

FAITH:

(*to Victor*) I won't look for you if you go.

VICTOR:

I said I'll be here. Go ahead.

MARK:

I'll make sure he stays right where he is.

VICTOR:

Yeah, he'll make sure I stay put. (*to Mark*) How you gonna do that?

MARK:

Won't be hard. What else you got to do?

FAITH:

I don't know this place.

MARK:

No way you can get lost. Place is only so big. Even if you get lost, you won't be lost.

VICTOR:

(*to Faith*) Go on.

FAITH:

Okay. (*she takes her shoes*) You'll be here when I get back? Both of you?

VICTOR:

We'll be here.

FAITH:

Wait for me.

MARK:

We will.

They watch her as she leaves, she stops, looks back. Victor waves, blows her a kiss and urges her on. Mark raises the bottle and she exits.

VICTOR:

Don't get lost. Hurry back. Love you. Etcetera, etcetera, etcetera.

MARK:

Etcetera, etcetera, etcetera? (*slight pause*) Where'd you find her, in a Cracker Jack box?

VICTOR:

Yeah. Ain't she great? Fuck, she's right on, man.

MARK:

She don't say much.

VICTOR:

I know. Tell me about it. Straight outta the bush.

MARK:

No. A bushy. Wow.

VICTOR:

Yeah. Can barely read a sign post. What do you think about that?

MARK:

Wow. That's something else. How old is she? What's she doing here, and does she have any sisters?

VICTOR:

I don't know. She's trying to find a life and I don't know.

MARK:

You're a lucky guy, Vic.

VICTOR:

I know.

MARK:

How come shit like that don't happen to me?

VICTOR:

I don't know.

MARK:

What you gonna do with her?

VICTOR:

I don't know. If I knew, I wouldn't tell you anyway. But we met at the bus depot, we talked all night and she balled my socks off. It was beautiful. I never felt like that before.

MARK:

You had a feeling?

VICTOR:

Sort of.

MARK:

How was it?

VICTOR:

Wasn't bad.

MARK:

Don't leave me, Vic.

VICTOR:

Don't talk like that.

MARK:

Can't help it. I'm already starting to feel alone, Vic.

VICTOR:

Dummy up. (*pause*) I'm gonna take her to meet my daddy.

MARK:

Why?

VICTOR:

Because it's the right thing to do.

MARK:

He'll eat her for breakfast, Vic.

VICTOR:

That old stiff? Not even on his best day.

MARK:

But you only met her last night.

VICTOR:

Yeah, but we clicked.

MARK:

(*pause*) Hey, look what's coming over here, Vic.

VICTOR:

Oh, blonde. Blonde good.

MARK:

No. Blonde bad.

VICTOR:

No. Blonde good.

MARK:

No.

VICTOR:

Yeah. Vic want to be blonde's robot.

MARK:

Oh, bad. Bad. Blonde bad.

VICTOR:

Bad? Why blonde bad?

MARK:

Blonde fuck-up Vic's gene pool.

VICTOR:

Oh, okay. Blonde bad.

MARK:

Yeah.

VICTOR:

But kinda good.

MARK:

Oh, bad

VICTOR:

Okay, dummy up with that shit now.

MARK:

(*drinks*) Ask you something, Vic?

VICTOR:

Fall back and let 'er rip, chum. Let 'er rip.

MARK:

(*drinks*) When you gonna get it into your head, that not every woman you see is interested in your small-dicked self?

VICTOR:

When I know it's not true.

MARK:

When?

VICTOR:

When I know it's not true, chum. When I know it's not true.

MARK:

(*chuckles*) I can't handle it, Vic. That's bad.

VICTOR:

Well, knock it off then.

MARK:

Yeah, okay. (*pause*) Oh hey, your old lady.

VICTOR:

Good. Good.

Faith comes on swinging her shoes by the laces.

VICTOR:

Hey, little girl, what's happening there?

FAITH:

Nothing.

VICTOR:

What you doing?

FAITH:

I soaked them too much.

VICTOR:

Oh. That's no good.

FAITH:

(*stops swinging the shoes*) Will you finish now?

VICTOR:

Finish what?

FAITH:

With my feet.

VICTOR:

Yeah, yeah. Sure thing.

FAITH:

Good. I didn't know if you would.

VICTOR:

You'll have to sit again.

FAITH:

(*to Mark*) You stayed too.

MARK:
Looks like it.

FAITH:
(*she sits – to Victor*) There's a man up there.

VICTOR:
Yeah? What's he doing?

FAITH:
Nothing.

VICTOR:
Nothing?

FAITH:
No.

VICTOR:
Well, what did he do?

FAITH:
Nothing. He's just there. Sleeping.

VICTOR:
In the can?

FAITH:
On the floor.

VICTOR:
On the floor?

FAITH:
On the floor.

VICTOR:
Drunk? Passed out?

FAITH:
I think so. I touched him.

VICTOR:

Where?

FAITH:

Up the stairs.

VICTOR:

No. I mean where did you touch him?

FAITH:

Right here. (*touches his chest*)

MARK:

Vic.

VICTOR:

(*to Mark*) Wait a minute. (*to Faith*) Then what happened?

FAITH:

Nothing.

VICTOR:

Nothing happened?

FAITH:

He said, "thank you".

VICTOR:

That's it?

FAITH:

He laughed and went back to sleep. I'm ready.

VICTOR:

For what? (*Faith points to her feet*) Oh yeah, okay. Tell you what I'm gonna do there, little girl. I'm gonna go take a look at this guy and let my friend here take over with your feet. How's that sound?

FAITH:

No good.

VICTOR:

Why not?

FAITH:

I want you.

VICTOR:

Oh, alright. (*to Mark*) *Adios amigo*. Go see this guy.

MARK:

What for?

VICTOR:

What for? Go see him.

MARK:

Ohhh.

VICTOR:

Take his pulse. See if he's alive.

MARK:

Good idea.

VICTOR:

Call an ambulance if he needs one.

MARK:

Right.

VICTOR:

Might be hurt.

MARK:

What else?

VICTOR:

I don't know. Fuck you're deadly. Think for yourself. Ask about his wife and kids or something. Check his wallet for ID.(*winks*) Find out where he lives.

MARK:

Like, to help him out, right?

VICTOR:

Of course, to help him out. What do you think? And don't take forever either.

MARK:

Won't take long at all, Vic.

Mark exits and Victor works on Faith's feet.

VICTOR:

I had enough. I can't do this anymore.

FAITH:

You don't like it now?

VICTOR:

Too much. Too much. (*pause*) Maybe you should put your shoes on.

FAITH:

They have to dry.

VICTOR:

Right.

FAITH:

I never did this before.

VICTOR:

What?

FAITH:

Put paint on my feet.

VICTOR:

No? Guess it's your lucky day.

FAITH:

Are you tired?

VICTOR:

Not a bit. I can go for days, little girl.

FAITH:

You look tired. You're shaking.

VICTOR:

I do that sometimes.

FAITH:

Why?

VICTOR:

I don't know. It happens.

FAITH:

You should stop.

VICTOR:

I can't help it.

FAITH:

Yes you can.

VICTOR:

What's happening here?

FAITH:

Where?

VICTOR:

Here. Right here.

FAITH:

Nothing.

VICTOR:

What is this thing?

FAITH:

What thing are you talking about?

VICTOR:

With us.

FAITH:

Do you want me to stop?

VICTOR:

Stop what? (*he shrugs*) What are you doing here?

FAITH:

I told you.

VICTOR:

You told me what?

FAITH:

Everything I could.

VICTOR:

You did?

FAITH:

You don't remember?

VICTOR:

Not all of it.

FAITH:

I should go.

VICTOR:

No. (*pause*) Stay... stay.

FAITH:

Are you sure?

VICTOR:

Of course I'm sure.

FAITH:

If you want me to go, I'll go. All you have to say is go.

VICTOR:

I can't do that.

FAITH:

You can.

VICTOR:

I know I can but I don't want to.

FAITH:

Good.

VICTOR:

Yeah? Why?

FAITH:

Because you're good… and I like you.

VICTOR:

Because I'm good and you like me. I don't know about that.

FAITH:

I do.

VICTOR:

No you don't. You don't know me at all.

FAITH:

I know you.

VICTOR:

Don't lie to me.

FAITH:

I don't lie.

VICTOR:

You're funny.

FAITH:

I'm funny? How am I funny?

VICTOR:

I don't know. You just are. There's something funny about you. You're different.

FAITH:

How am I different?

VICTOR:

If I knew I'd tell you.

FAITH:

Your friend is done.

VICTOR:

No he isn't.

FAITH:

He's done.

VICTOR:

(*pause*) I'm going to see someone later.

FAITH:

I know.

VICTOR:

No you don't.

FAITH:

Okay, I don't.

VICTOR:

I want you to come with me.

FAITH:

I know.

VICTOR:

Don't say you know when you don't. Don't do that.

FAITH:

Okay. Here he is.

Mark enters.

VICTOR:

(*to Mark*) So?

MARK:

What?

VICTOR:

What's the story with our sleepy friend?

MARK:

He's a little under the weather right now, Vic.

VICTOR:

What's wrong with him?

MARK:

Hard to say. I think life's been hard on him, Vic.

VICTOR:

That's sad.

MARK:

It's terrible. He gave me his wallet though.

VICTOR:

That was nice of him.

MARK:

He has a lot of heart, Vic.

VICTOR:

I'll say.

MARK:

All he wanted was someone to talk to. So I talked to him and he gave me his wallet. Surprised the shit outta me, man.

VICTOR:

Sometimes that's all it takes. A few kind words and people will give you whatever they have.

MARK:

That is so true, Vic. (*tosses the wallet to Victor*) Some people really know how to give. Remember the big bald guy and his little black book?

VICTOR:

Mr. Clean.

MARK:

(*to Faith*) Gave us each ten bucks for nothing.

VICTOR:

That was too wild, chum. (*inspects the wallet*) Genuine cowhide. Made in India. What the fuck next?

MARK:

What did he say to you, Vic?

VICTOR:

Asked if we were working. (*shakes out the wallet – picks up a piece of folded paper*)

MARK:

What did you tell him?

VICTOR:

Told him if I was working, I wouldn't be wasting my time talking to him. (*unfolds the paper*) You were there.

MARK:

(*to Faith*) Asks for our names, writes them down in his little black book and forks us over ten bucks a piece. You figure it out.

VICTOR:

(*reading from the paper*) "Your wife called. She wants house. If any problems, call lawyer." Fucking memo from hell, man. Some guys just can't let go. (*crumples the paper and throws it at Mark*) Poor bastard.

MARK:

Why would a person dish out money like that, Vic?

VICTOR:

I don't know. (*looks in the wallet*)

MARK:

Bothers me, man. One of them things that don't leave me alone.

VICTOR:

Why would you let something like that bother you? If anyone deserves ten bucks for standing on a corner it's us.

MARK:

Never felt good about it, Vic. Didn't seem right.

VICTOR:

What do you care? You ate for a week. (*slight pause*) Probably the guy sinned heavily and was out looking for points. Covering his bases or some fucking thing like that. What we got here? Two two-dollar bills way down in the corner. Come on out boys. No use hiding. (*takes out the bills*)

MARK:

(*to Faith*) Why do you think he did it?

FAITH:

Maybe you were pitiful.

VICTOR:

(*as he puts the bills in his pocket and the wallet in Mark's back pocket*) Yeah, maybe you were pitiful.

MARK:

You were there too.

VICTOR:

Well, that's okay because there's a difference between looking pitiful and being pitiful. Me, I can look pitiful if I have to. You, on the other hand, don't have no choice in the matter. Comes natural for you. Know what I'm saying?

MARK:

No. I think we're pretty much the same, Vic.

VICTOR:

Well, let me put it to you like this: Shut the fuck up now, okay.

MARK:

(*to Faith*) What the hell do you see in this guy?

FAITH:

Lots.

MARK:

Lots? Lots of what? Must be keeping it to himself.

FAITH:

He'll be okay.

MARK:

So what you're saying is he's a pig now but he'll be a better pig later. That what you're saying?

FAITH:

No.

VICTOR:

(*to Faith*) What you talking about?

FAITH:

You.

VICTOR:

Well, stop it. I hate it when people talk about me right in front of me.

FAITH:

I thought you'd like it.

VICTOR:

Makes me feel like shit. It's worse than people talking about me behind my back.

MARK:

Gotta remember that.

FAITH:

Me too.

VICTOR:

(*to Faith*) Your foot dry yet?

FAITH:

It's dry.

VICTOR:

What about your shoes?

FAITH:

Almost.

VICTOR:

Almost is close enough for me, little girl. Know what we're doing?

FAITH:

I know.

VICTOR:

What?

FAITH:

Going to visit?

VICTOR:

That's exactly right, little girl. I wanna see this guy before it gets too fucking dark.

MARK:

Say the word, Vic. I'm ready.

VICTOR:

Where do you think you're going?

MARK:

With you guys.

VICTOR:

Not today. Maybe you should sit this one out.

FAITH:

He can come.

VICTOR:

What?

FAITH:

It's okay. There's always four.

VICTOR:

Oh yeah, right, there's always four. (*to Mark*) Fuck, you're a heavy load.

MARK:

You won't even know I'm there, Vic.

VICTOR:

You gonna put your shoes on or what?

FAITH:

I'm not wearing them wet.

VICTOR:

I don't blame you.

FAITH:

I'll carry them.

VICTOR:

Your shoes.

Faith ties shoes together and slings them over her shoulder. Mark takes a drink and tucks the bottle in his pants. He takes the wallet from his back pocket, wipes it and tosses it away. Victor lights a cig- arette and leads the way whistling, "Guantanamera".

FAITH:

Don't whistle.

VICTOR:

Why not?

FAITH:

It's not good.

VICTOR:

Why?

FAITH:

Just isn't.

VICTOR:

(*whistles – to Faith*) Okay.

MARK:

I like that tune, Vic. Makes me feel like a refugee humping through the bush.

VICTOR:

No bush around here.

MARK:

Nothing here but nothing, Vic.

VICTOR:

And someday it's all gonna be yours.

MARK:

Thank you, Vic.

VICTOR:

It's alright.

FAITH:

(*to Victor*) Do you like living in this place?

VICTOR:

What place?

FAITH:

> This place.

VICTOR:

> Here? In town?

FAITH:

> Yeah.

VICTOR:

> Yeah, I don't mind it. I'm a city boy.

FAITH:

> Why do you like it?

VICTOR:

> I don't know. (*to himself*) Always been good to me.

MARK:

> (*to Faith*) Where do you come from?

FAITH:

> Over there.

MARK:

> Over there? Where over there? Across the ocean?

FAITH:

> No. Way over there. Far.

MARK:

> That narrows it down don't it, Vic?

VICTOR:

> Right down to the bone, chum.

MARK:

> (*to Faith*) So where's far? Saigon? Fond Du Lac? Kansas?

FAITH:

> You don't need to know.

VICTOR:

Don't think it's any of your business anyway.

MARK:

Just trying to make a little friendly conversation, Vic.

FAITH:

(*to Mark*) You like it here too?

MARK:

Me? Yeah, I like it. I love living in the city. I love living in the city.

FAITH:

Why?

MARK:

(*slight pause*) Don't know. Never really thought about it. Hey Vic, why do we love living in the city?

VICTOR:

How the fuck should I know?

MARK:

Well, gimme a drag then.

VICTOR:

Find your own smokes.

MARK:

Vic, you're not sharing. That's a bad thing, Vic. That's bad.

VICTOR:

Fuck. Here. (*gives him the smoke*) Suck it till your lungs bleed.

MARK:

Oh good. Vic change mind. That's good. (*slight pause*) Take a short cut, Vic?

VICTOR:

No short cuts around here. That's bad. Short cuts bad. (*to Faith*) How you feeling?

FAITH:

Good.

VICTOR:

Good. You're not scared?

FAITH:

No.

VICTOR:

Don't lie to me.

FAITH:

Should I be?

VICTOR:

No.

FAITH:

Why did you ask?

VICTOR:

Just wondering.

MARK:

You gonna tell her the rules, Vic?

FAITH:

Rules?

VICTOR:

Few things to keep in mind.

FAITH:

Okay.

VICTOR:

Like when we get there, don't say nothing about women's rights or global warming or none of that shit. alright?

FAITH:

Why? Is he like a... a... a bad ass? Is that how you say it?

VICTOR:

Yeah right. Bad ass. That's right. So be yourself and don't talk too much.

MARK:

And try not to look like you're thinking either. Right, Vic?

VICTOR:

Right.

FAITH:

(*to Victor*) Be myself?

VICTOR:

That's right. Be yourself.

FAITH:

Right on. Is that how?

VICTOR:

Right on. Right. You're learning.

FAITH:

I know.

VICTOR:

You're quick.

FAITH:

Right on.

VICTOR:

(*to Mark*) She's quick huh, bud?

MARK:

Fast, Vic, fast. Fast. Fast.

FAITH:

Right on. (*slight pause*) Deadly. Far out. Up yours. Fuck you, man. (*covers her mouth*)

VICTOR:

No. That's good. Good. Good.

MARK:

(*to Faith*) Beautiful. It's in there. Let it out.

FAITH:

No. That's all.

VICTOR:

You were doing good.

FAITH:

I don't like to swear too much.

VICTOR:

Try it. You'll like it.

FAITH:

(*slight pause*) Fuck you, man.

VICTOR:

Yeah. You're doing it.

FAITH:

Fuck you, man.

VICTOR:

Deadly. (*to Mark*) She's got it. I think she's got it.

MARK:

Perfect. You're a good teacher, Vic.

FAITH:

Fuck you, man... and your horse too.

VICTOR:

The horse you rode in on.

FAITH:

What?

VICTOR:

The horse you rode in on. Fuck you and the horse you rode in on.

FAITH:

Oh. Okay.

VICTOR:

Say it.

FAITH:

No.

VICTOR:

Come on. Say it.

FAITH:

That's all for me.

VICTOR:

Aww. Don't be a quitter.

MARK:

Bottle's killing me, man. (*undoes his pants and takes out the bottle*)

FAITH:

Oh.

VICTOR:

Behave yourself.

MARK:

Pants are too tight. Need some relief. Hold onto this. (*holds out the bottle to Victor*)

VICTOR:

Fuck no. That's your shit. You hold onto it.

MARK:

(*to Faith*) You take it.

FAITH:

Okay.

She takes the bottle. Mark does up his pants, tucks in his shirt. Faith gives him the bottle back and they move on.

MARK:

Thanks, babe. You're the best thing that ever happened to me.

VICTOR:

Hey, watch your fucking mouth and find your own damn girl, boy.

MARK:

Just fucking with you, Vic.

VICTOR:

Well don't do that.

At Percy's house.

VICTOR:

(*to Faith*) You okay?

FAITH:

Yeah.

VICTOR:

Okay. You might wanna take a few deep breaths and think about the good things in life before we go in there, little girl.

FAITH:

You think so?

VICTOR:

Yeah.

FAITH:

Okay. (*she breathes deep and pauses*) Good?

VICTOR:

Good.

FAITH:

(*tugs on Victor's sleeve*) Don't call me that anymore.

VICTOR:

What?

FAITH:

Little girl.

VICTOR:

Why not?

FAITH:

Because I'm not one.

VICTOR:

Fine.

MARK:

Hey Vic, what do you think it is that makes a person go bad?

VICTOR:

(*at Percy's door*) How the fuck should I know? Could be anything. Poverty… cops… snow… the moon… show-biz. Take your fucking pick.

MARK:

Good answer, Vic. Good answer. Don't help me none, but it's a good answer.

VICTOR:

Hey, Percy! Percy, you alive in there or what?! (*shrugs – to himself*) This fucking guy deaf or something?

In Percy's house.

MARK:

Jesus H. Fucking Christ and his half-brother Ned, Vic. What is that?

VICTOR:

Something dying.

MARK:

Fuck this. Let's go party till my momma cries, Vic.

VICTOR:

Too late.

PERCY:

Well, what the fuck do you know, it's sweet Vicky.

VICTOR:

Nice to see you too.

PERCY:

No kidding? Look at this, the gang's all here. Well, shuffle on in, you're blocking my fucking view. What we got here? A female even. Good to see someone's on the fucking ball.

VICTOR:

Faith, Percy. Percy, Faith.

PERCY:

(*to Faith*) Faith, huh? I'm pleased. (*to Victor*) Now what would you guys being doing with a little faith? (*to Faith*) Who do you belong to?

FAITH:

What?

PERCY:

What. (*to Victor*) Girl speaks right up. (*to Faith*) I said, who do you belong to?

FAITH:

Me.

PERCY:

Me?

FAITH:

No. I belong to no one.

PERCY:

A free agent. That's allowed.

VICTOR:

So what you up to, Percy?

PERCY:

I was sitting in that chair having one of the purest thoughts I've ever had, till you walked in and pissed all over it. (*to Faith*) Make yourself at home. Have a sit down and tell me what you're doing with a couple pukes like these two here.

FAITH:

Okay.

VICTOR:

(*to Percy*) Kinda fucking close in here, don't you think? Why don't you open a window and get some fresh air happening. Fuck me.

MARK:

That would be good.

PERCY:

I like it close. Makes me feel warm all over. You don't like it, there's the door. Don't be afraid to use it.

VICTOR:

No fear here. Hey, it was just a suggestion.

PERCY:

When I want your suggestions I'll ask for them. That way you don't have to go around wasting them. How's that sound?

VICTOR:

Whatever.

PERCY:

So what's shaking? You're not being bad are you? God, I hope not. So when you going home?

VICTOR:

Give yourself a chance to get sick of us at least.

PERCY:

I'm almost there already.

VICTOR:

No use offering you a drink then, I guess.

PERCY:

Well that's a different story. Please stay. My home is your home and all that shit. You drinking again?

VICTOR:

Fuck no. The world could burn and I wouldn't take another fucking drink. Mark here has a bottle.

PERCY:

(*to Victor*) I feel sorry for you. (*to Mark*) You, you're my favourite non-Native guy in the whole wide world. And I'm not saying that just to make you feel good either.

MARK:

Didn't think so. How you doing, Percy? Been a long time.

PERCY:

Don't seem like it.

MARK:

How's your general constipation these days?

PERCY:

What's that?

VICTOR:

(*to Mark*) Constitution, pal.

MARK:

Sorry, Percy.

PERCY:

Don't be. I understand. It's gotta be fucking tough being you. We gonna get into that or not?

MARK:

You want a taste?

PERCY:

You know it.

VICTOR:

What the hell happened to your head?

Mark pours a drink

PERCY:

I got hurt. (*to Mark*) You're beautiful.

MARK:

I know.

VICTOR:

I can see you got hurt. How?

PERCY:

Best way I know.

VICTOR:

How's that?

PERCY:

Took a little risk.

VICTOR:

Was it worth it?

PERCY:

We'll have to wait and see.

VICTOR:

What did you do?

PERCY:

I can't say.

VICTOR:

Why not?

PERCY:

Cause you'll tell everyone and their fucking enemy.

VICTOR:

No way. As if.

PERCY:

You'll ruin it.

VICTOR:

I can't see it happening.

PERCY:

Don't want my name ending up on some lieutenant's desk.

VICTOR:

Fuck.

PERCY:

Just kidding. I know you better than that. Can I trust you with this?

VICTOR:

Of course.

PERCY:

Won't get around?

VICTOR:

Not by me it won't.

PERCY:

You sure?

VICTOR:

Forget it. I don't want to hear about it.

PERCY:

Okay, I'll tell you. I hocked my TV last month.

VICTOR:

Oh my God. You're lucky to be alive.

PERCY:

You gonna listen to this or not?

VICTOR:

I'm listening.

MARK:

Me too.

PERCY:

Okay. I hocked my TV. Monday, I went to get it out and this little fucking chink don't believe I paid. I know I paid one of them fuckers, but I never seen this guy before and right away the wheels are turning.

VICTOR:

Yeah?

PERCY:

Oh yeah. So I tell this guy to go fuck himself and I pick up my TV, I tell him it's mine and see you later. He starts gritting his teeth and what not. Fuck, thought he was gonna piss his pants for Christ sake.

VICTOR:

No.

PERCY:

Yeah. He's screaming, no no, TV stay. You no pay. You leave. You bad man. You fucking right I'm leaving, pal. This is no fucking way to do business. Immigrant cocksucker eating up my tax dollars. Fuck him.

VICTOR:

That's bad.

MARK:

Bad. Immigrants bad, man.

VICTOR:

You don't know the half of it, pal.

PERCY:

Fucking pain in the ass. But then it comes to me and I say to myself, here's your chance. I'm walking out the door with my TV and I can hear this fucking guy running up behind me. He had just enough time to close my eyes and the little fucker jumps eight feet in the air and comes down. Bang! Elbow right in the fucking head.

VICTOR:

Jesus.

MARK:

Sounds like you fucked with the Wong guy, Percy.

PERCY:

Cute. It was good. Hard but good. Room fulla witnesses. Lotta oh's and ah's. All that shit.

VICTOR:

Yeah?

PERCY:

Definitely.

MARK:

He knock you out?

PERCY:

Not really. He wobbled me but I didn't go down. Had a little headache. That's fuck all. A few stitches. Big deal. Talked to my lawyer and he says I got a real good case.

VICTOR:

Oh, good.

MARK:

Yeah, good. Good case... good.

VICTOR:

Elbow in the head… bad.

MARK:

Yeah. Witnesses are good. Lawyer good?

VICTOR:

Lawyer… good.

MARK:

Okay.

VICTOR:

(*to Percy*) How good a case you got?

PERCY:

I can win.

MARK:

Winning is good.

VICTOR:

Yeah. (*to Percy*) Cash settlement?

PERCY:

You fucking know it.

MARK:

Oh, cash settlement... good.

VICTOR:

Yeah.

MARK:

System good.

VICTOR:

No. System bad.

MARK:

System bad?

VICTOR:

Yeah.

MARK:

No.

VICTOR:

Yeah.

MARK:

No. System works… good.

VICTOR:

Okay. (*to Percy*) How much you think you'll get?

PERCY:

I asked the very same fucking question. But talking to this guy is like talking to a piece of fucking cardboard.

MARK:

Oh, cardboard lawyers... bad.

VICTOR:

Bad.

PERCY:

Legal Aid prick. "How much?" I ask him. "Not much," he says. Well how much is not much? "Not much," he says. Not much. Fuck. So I tell him long as it's enough for a cow and a block of salt, I'll be satisfied.

MARK:

Oh, cows are good.

VICTOR:

Yeah. Salt's good too.

PERCY:

Everything works out, I'll be back on the rez by fall watching my cow grow.

MARK:

Oh, cow grow... good.

VICTOR:

Beef's good.

MARK:

Ground round good.

VICTOR:

Steak good.

MARK:

Ribs good.

VICTOR:

Neck bones good.

MARK:

Neck bones?

FAITH:

Good.

PERCY:

What the fuck you guys on?

VICTOR:

Nothing.

PERCY:

Come on, cut me in.

VICTOR:

I don't have nothing.

PERCY:

(*to Mark*) You?

MARK:

Don't look at me.

PERCY:

No drugs?

VICTOR:

Not me.

MARK:

All I have is what's in your hand, Percy.

PERCY:

No kidding?

MARK:

Kid you not, man. That's it.

PERCY:

Fuck it. Beggars can't be choosers.

VICTOR:

That's what I say. (to Percy) Hey, where's what's-her-name?

MARK:

Thought there was something missing.

PERCY:

(*to Victor*) If it's alright with you, what's-her-name don't live here no more.

MARK:

That's rough, man.

PERCY:

Fuck all rough about that.

VICTOR:

No?

PERCY:

Fuck no. It's a part of life. Think I need a woman to make me… whole or whatever the fuck it is? Fuck.

VICTOR:

Guess not.

MARK:

So, you're dogging it.

PERCY:

You know it.

VICTOR:

That's bad.

PERCY:

Yeah well, we weren't seeing eye to eye and I had to kick her out.

VICTOR:

You gotta go, you gotta go.

PERCY:

(*slight pause*) Actually, she left. But I told her to get the hell out as she was going through the door. I got my pride.

VICTOR:

That's the main thing.

PERCY:

You fucking know it.

VICTOR:

What the hell's the matter with you guys now? (*to Faith*) Come sit here. (*she sits beside him*)

PERCY:

Same old thing. She hated the way I never did nothing for her and... I hated the way she hated it. We never talked about it, we just hated each other for it.

VICTOR:

That'll do it.

PERCY:

Fuck it. I'm better off.

VICTOR

Yeah?

PERCY:

Oh yeah. No one to worry about. Just me and Moses here now.

VICTOR:

Nice and quiet?

PERCY:

Just the way I like it. (*pause*) I don't know where she gets off saying I never did nothing for her. Last year she OD's and what do I do? Two days straight I'm holding her hand, praying. No shit. I said, Lord, please don't take her, she's not ready. She might be crazy as a shit house rat, but she's never seen Rogers Pass or the Calgary Tower or nothing. What the fuck does she do? She pulls through and she's been torturing me ever since.

VICTOR:

You never told me that.

PERCY:

I just did. Fuck it. Who needs it? I don't.

VICTOR:

You seem to be handling it okay. (*to Mark*) Don't you think?

MARK:

Shit yeah.

PERCY:

(*to Victor*) You think so?

VICTOR:

Like a pro.

PERCY:

Well, what the fuck am I supposed to do, lay down and die? (*slight pause*) All I know is you gotta be careful about what you ask for. What am I doing dumping all this shit on you? What are you doing here?

VICTOR:

What?

PERCY:

You heard me.

VICTOR:

What do you mean?

PERCY:

I mean, what the fuck are you doing here?

MARK:

We come to show you Faith, give you a drink and watch some TV, Percy. That about cover it, Vic?

VICTOR:

That's about it.

PERCY:

Well you're shit outta luck. Tube don't work worth shit. Ole what's-her-name tried taking it and I threw myself on it. Broke something deep inside. Can't do nothing now except ache for Oprah. Fucking know it all.

VICTOR:

Come on, don't be bad mouthing Oprah like that. You don't even know her.

PERCY:

Feel like I do.

MARK:

Man, I love the way she wrinkles her nose when she fakes a smile.

PERCY:

No kidding? That's the one thing about her that makes me sick. Turns my fucking stomach when she does that. Other than that, she can darken my door any ol' time. (*to Victor*) Now cut the crap and tell me what you're doing here.

VICTOR:

We told you. We come to watch some TV.

PERCY:

Bullshit. That's bullshit.

VICTOR:

I need a reason to come see you now?

PERCY:

Might help. It's Saturday night, boy, shouldn't you be out trying to ruin someone's life?

VICTOR:

Always time for that.

PERCY:

You never know. Mark, you stingy prick, be a good boy and give us another swallow.

MARK:

Help yourself, Percy.

PERCY:

That's what I like to hear. (*pours a drink – to Victor*) I gotta tell you something. You have to get out there and hustle, boy. I'm not getting any younger and I'm gonna need something for my golden years.

VICTOR:

I'm out there every fucking day, man.

MARK:

He is, Percy. He's out there every fucking day, man. Like clockwork.

PERCY:

(*to Victor*) I'd believe it if you had something to show for it. Shouldn't waste your time coming around here.

VICTOR:

Why not?

PERCY:

Because I'm telling you not to. Christ, you're young. You should be out there pillaging at least. What's the matter with you? You know how to score. You're not that ugly that you can't find some ol' rich broad to take care of you… and me.

VICTOR:

Got all the broad I need sitting right here.

PERCY:

That so?

VICTOR:

That's right. (*to Faith*) Right?

FAITH:

What?

VICTOR:

You and me all the way, right?

FAITH:

Okay.

VICTOR:

(*to Percy*) See?

PERCY:

Fair enough. Good to see your not afraid to make a fucking mistake.

VICTOR:

No fear here, man.

PERCY:

That's good. It's the only way you're ever gonna learn. (*to Mark*) Ain't that right, dick nose?

MARK:

Me?

PERCY:

You see any other dick noses around here?

MARK:

No.

PERCY:

There you go.

MARK:

I don't know, Percy. I fucked up a lot and haven't learned sweet fuck all yet.

PERCY:

Well, I think you must be the exception to the rule.

MARK:

You might be right, Percy.

PERCY:

I know I'm right.

MARK:

I keep right on doing it too. Wish I knew what the fuck is wrong with me.

PERCY:

Probably you don't know any fucking better.

MARK:

That could be.

VICTOR:

(*to Faith*) Where you going?

FAITH:

Over there.

VICTOR:

Don't go too far.

FAITH:

I won't.

PERCY:

(*to Victor*) What's she got against shoes?

VICTOR:

Not too much you can do about wet shoes. Let'em dry, I guess.

MARK:

Yeah. Dry shoes are good, man.

PERCY:

Bet your ass dry shoes are good. Can't go slopping around in wet shoes for fuck sake.

VICTOR:

That's what I say.

PERCY:

Give us a good smoke then. Been dying for a good smoke all day.

VICTOR:

What's wrong with yours?

PERCY:

Tastes like shit and makes me cough.

VICTOR:

Yeah?

PERCY:

Yeah. Hack around all day smoking them things. Open my eyes in the morning, first thing I do is cough. All day, all night, all I do is cough.

VICTOR:

That's too bad.

PERCY:

Tell me about it (*coughs*).

VICTOR:

That's too bad. You should quit. (*gives him a smoke*) Smoking can kill you.

PERCY:

So can a bus. You fucking quit.

VICTOR:

Not today. Maybe later.

PERCY:

(*lights a cigarette*) So, what is it this time, love or lust?

VICTOR:

It's too soon to tell.

PERCY:

How does she taste?

VICTOR:

What?

PERCY:

You heard me.

VICTOR:

What the fuck kinda question is that to be asking me?

PERCY:

It's a fair question. You two are together aren't you? If she's with him, too, I'll shit.

VICTOR:

Orange Crush. She tastes like Orange Crush.

PERCY:

No shit? Had a broad in Vancouver, swear to God tasted like old fashioned doughnuts.

VICTOR:

Deadly.

PERCY:

Delicious.

VICTOR:

Yeah?

PERCY:

Oh, I don't even want to talk about it.

VICTOR:

Do I know her?

PERCY:

Forget about it. She'd spank you, boy.

VICTOR:

Yeah? Where does she live?

PERCY:

Sick fuck.

VICTOR:

Thanks, dad.

PERCY:

She was a tough ol' broad. Real good looking too. Looked like Veronica from the Archie comics.

VICTOR:

Yeah?

PERCY:

Nice. Very nice. We did a thing in Burnaby once. We're celebrating and a couple fucking hoods walk in the joint looking for me. I'm buying drinks and I see them coming. I know these guys and what they can do, and I'm thinking, this is it. I'm shaking. I mean, I'm really shaking. So she walks up real casual and puts a piece to the one guy's head and says, you got three seconds to stay or live.

VICTOR:

No.

MARK:

Bad broad.

VICTOR:

No kidding.

PERCY:

She was a tough fucking broad, I told you. Solid. Too fucking solid.

VICTOR:

Right on.

PERCY:

Oh yeah. Saved my ass more than once.

MARK:

Did she do it?

PERCY:

Didn't have to. Everyone did as they were told and left.

VICTOR:

I guess so.

PERCY:

Wouldn't you?

VICTOR:

You'd never see me there no more. (*to Mark*) What about you?

MARK:

Me, I'd probably stick around and get my brains blown out by a beautiful broad from Burnaby.

PERCY:

You're kind of a sad fucking case, aren't you?

MARK:

No. I'm a happy case, Percy. Sounds like the woman could handle herself.

PERCY:

She was tough as fucking Charles Bronson. Didn't look like him though. Fuck she was gorgeous. Blew a bundle on her too.

VICTOR:

Was she worth it?

PERCY:

Every fucking nickel.

VICTOR:

That's good.

PERCY:

Lot better at the time, I tell you.

VICTOR:

No doubt.

PERCY:

Fucking broads.

VICTOR:

Love 'em.

PERCY:

Yeah.

MARK:

Me too.

PERCY:

(*to Mark*) Me too. You're lucky if you get to stroke your neighbours cat, you ugly bastard you.

MARK:

That's it, Percy. You're cut off.

PERCY:

Yeah?

MARK:

No.

PERCY:

You had me worried for a second there.

MARK:

Sorry, Percy.

PERCY:

Fuck that. There's no such thing as sorry. Sorry's just a word between shit and syphilis.

MARK:

Yeah?

PERCY:

Look it up. And give me another drink while you're at it.

MARK:

(*pours a drink*) That good?

PERCY:

Perfect. (*pause*) How's your dad doing these days, Mark?

MARK:

I don't know.

PERCY:

You don't know? What kinda son are you?

MARK:

The good kind.

PERCY:

The good kind. What kinda son doesn't know how his father is?

VICTOR:

He told you. The good kind.

MARK

(*to Percy*) What can I say? There's a lot of negative shit flying off that guy and most of it's aimed at me. So like, you know, fuck it.

PERCY:

You should be ashamed of yourself. Guys like you should be shot and pissed on.

MARK:

Okay.

PERCY:

No, really. You should be really ashamed.

MARK:

I am. I am. I'm feeling great shame, Percy. Hey, I can't handle this right now. Bringing back too many bad memories. (*to Victor*) Think I'll take a little stroll and see how our Faith's doing.

VICTOR:

Our Faith?

MARK:

Sorry, Vic. Your Faith.

VICTOR:

That's better.

Mark goes to Faith.

PERCY:

(*to Victor*) You figure it out yet?

VICTOR:

(*watching Mark and Faith – to Percy*) What?

Two simultaneous conversations begin. One between Mark and Faith and the other between Victor and Percy. (except where indicated)

MARK:

What you doing? You making friends? You figure out what you're doing here?

FAITH:

I think so.

VICTOR:

We told you.

MARK:

That's Moses.

PERCY:

I don't buy it. Wait, don't tell me. You need a place to stay.

FAITH:

He's nice. I like him.

VICTOR:

How did you know?

MARK:

(*to Faith*) I think he's a girl. (*to Percy*) Hey Percy, is Moses a boy or a girl?

PERCY:

(*to Victor*) You have that homeless look. (*to Mark*) Who wants to know?

VICTOR:

Yeah?

MARK:

We do.

PERCY:

(*to Mark*) She's a girl. (*to Victor*) What happened?

MARK:

(*to himself*) That's what I thought. (*to Faith*) See if she bites.

VICTOR:

I lost my place.

FAITH:

What?

PERCY:

How'd you manage that?

MARK:

Put your finger in her mouth.

VICTOR:

Some asshole stole my check.

FAITH:

No.

PERCY:

You weren't waiting by the mailbox? What the fuck's the matter with you?

MARK:

You scared?

VICTOR:

I slipped.

FAITH:

No. It's not nice.

PERCY:

That's no fucking excuse. You break my heart with them bullshit excuses. Well, you deserve whatever you get and you get the porch.

MARK:

Put her on her back.

VICTOR:

Thanks, dad.

FAITH:

No. That's a mean thing to do. She'll get mad.

PERCY:

What's happening with you and that girl?

MARK:

So what?

VICTOR:

What girl?

FAITH:

I can't do that to her.

PERCY:

She staying with you?

MARK:

Sure you can.

VICTOR:

I don't know.

FAITH:

No.

PERCY:

Either way it's a hundred bucks a month. And on time. None of this I'll pay you in a couple days bullshit. You get things straightened out with your worker and we'll talk more if things... fluctuate.

MARK:

You can. Believe me.

VICTOR:

Sounds fair.

FAITH:

Talk to her.

PERCY:

That's more than fair. You won't get a deal like that anywhere else.

MARK:

What?

VICTOR:

That's true.

FAITH:

Say something to her.

PERCY:

Bet your ass it's true.

MARK:

No. I don't talk to reptiles. Sorry.

VICTOR:

It's all settled then?

FAITH:

Try it.

PERCY:

How long is this gonna last?

MARK:

I'm too shy for that shit, Faith.

VICTOR:

Just long enough to get myself established.

FAITH:

No, you're not.

PERCY:

Shit, I could be waiting five or ten years for that to happen. I don't have that kinda time.

MARK:

Okay. You talked me into it. (*to Moses*) Hi. (*laughs to Faith*) Good enough?

VICTOR:

As if.

FAITH:

More than that.

PERCY:

As if nothing. I'll be an old bag of bones before that happens. Moses there moves faster than you. You're no fucking go getter, that's for sure.

MARK:

(*clears his throat*) Kitchy-koo, you little bastard. How's it hanging? (*laughs to Fatih*) Okay?

VICTOR:

Whatever.

FAITH:

Say good things to her.

PERCY:

Hey you two, what's going on over there?

The two simultaneous conversations end.

MARK:

What?

PERCY:

You heard me.

MARK:

Nothing bad, Percy. We're just talking to Moses.

PERCY:

Oh. That's fuck all. I do it all the time. Just don't piss her off. (*to Victor*) You're not worried about your woman straying?

VICTOR:

Me? Not at all. That's the last thing I'm worried about. (*he goes to Mark and Faith – to Faith*) How you doing?

FAITH:

Good.

VICTOR:

(*to Mark*) You behaving yourself?

MARK:

Vic.

VICTOR:

Just checking. (*to Faith*) You need anything?

FAITH:

Not right now.

VICTOR:

You hungry?

FAITH:

No.

VICTOR:

A little bit?

FAITH:

Maybe.

VICTOR:

Percy, you got any food? My honey's hungry.

PERCY:

We can't have that. Feed her.

VICTOR:

What?

PERCY:

There's a Mr. Big in the freezer.

VICTOR:

(*to Faith*) You want a chocolate bar?

FAITH:

Do you?

VICTOR:

I can take it or leave it. Don't matter to me.

FAITH:

We can share.

Percy goes to the three.

PERCY:

What's going on here? Who's hungry? (*to Faith*) This fucking guy starving you?

FAITH:

No.

PERCY:

(*to Victor*) Get her something to eat. What's the matter with you?

VICTOR:

Mark, do us a favour.

MARK:

What?

VICTOR:

Take yourself to the kitchen and find us a Mr. Big candy bar in the freezer.

MARK:

Why me?

VICTOR:

Because I'm asking you. You're my pal. We're buds. Fellow dudes. Bro's and all that shit.

MARK:

No.

VICTOR:

No?

MARK:

No. I'm feeling bad, Vic.

VICTOR:

Mark feel bad?

MARK:

Yeah.

VICTOR:

Why?

MARK:

Mark feel like Vic's unpaid butler.

VICTOR:

That's bad.

MARK:

Yeah.

VICTOR:

Mark is not Vic's butler.

MARK:

No?

VICTOR:

No. Mark is Mark's own man.

MARK:

Oh, good.

VICTOR:

Yeah good. Now fetch candy bar, my boy. Okay. (*Mark exits*)

PERCY:

(*to Victor*) You fucking guys retarded or what?

VICTOR:

No.

PERCY:

What the fuck's the matter with you then?

VICTOR:

I don't know. Nothing.

PERCY:

Nothing my ass. Ask me I think you both need a little fine tuning.

VICTOR:

No. We don't need none of that.

PERCY:

Yeah, I think so. Couple sociable cracks across the head would have you talking right again.

VICTOR:

No.

PERCY:

Maybe not. You'd probably enjoy it.

VICTOR:

(*to Faith*) That's not true.

PERCY:

(*to Faith*) You two look like you're hitting it off.

VICTOR:

We are.

PERCY:

Not you. Her and Moses. (*to Faith*) Usually the little fucker don't take to strangers. You something special?

FAITH:

No. There's something wrong with her.

PERCY:

What's the matter with her?

FAITH:

She might be getting sick.

PERCY:

How do you know this?

FAITH:

I just look at her and I know.

PERCY:

No shit?

FAITH:

No shit.

Mark comes in with a candy bar sliced and on a plate.

MARK:

(*to Faith*) Here you go. For your dining pleasure, a fine mix of nuts, glucose and uh… plastic.

VICTOR:

Thanks. (*takes the plate – to Faith*) Open up. (*feeds her a slice of candy bar*)

PERCY:

Mark, you're going to make someone a wonderful wife someday.

MARK:

Don't get your hopes up, Percy. (*laughs – to Faith*) Good stuff?

FAITH:

Not really.

VICTOR:

You'll get used to it.

FAITH:

I don't think so.

MARK:

I don't think so either.

VICTOR:

Who asked you?

PERCY:

(*to Faith*) Need a little something to wash that down? (*offers her his drink*)

FAITH:

No.

PERCY:

(*to Victor*) What's that green shit?

VICTOR:

What green shit?

PERCY:

On her foot. You got some green shit on your foot there, Faith. What is that? Mold?

FAITH:

Paint.

MARK:

Mold? (*laughs*)

PERCY:

(to Mark) What the fuck you laughing at? Was an honest mistake. From where I am, looks like a bad case of trench foot. (*Mark laughs – to Victor*) What the fuck's the matter with this guy?

VICTOR

Beats me.

FAITH:

(*to Victor*) I don't want anymore.

PERCY:

(*to Faith*) I don't blame you. Never eat them myself. Moses there likes the odd treat.

FAITH:

It's not good for her.

PERCY:

If it's good enough for the kid down the block, it's good enough for her.

FAITH:

No. She needs good food.

PERCY:

What, steak? I can barely afford to feed myself for fuck sake.

MARK:

Fuck, I'm hammered, Vic.

VICTOR:

Drink some more.

MARK:

Yeah. Hey, Percy.

PERCY:

What?

MARK:

How's your head?

VICTOR:

(*to Mark*) Don't.

PERCY:

Not too bad now. Why?

MARK:

Give me some then.

VICTOR:

Holy shit.

PERCY:

(*chuckling – to Victor*) This fucking guy.

MARK:

(*laughing*) Sorry, Percy. Been dying to say that all night. I had to say it.

PERCY:

That's okay. (*to Victor and Faith*) I can take a joke. You think I can't take a fucking joke? I can take a joke.

MARK:

Really?

PERCY:

Really.

MARK:

Well fuck off then. (*laughs*)

VICTOR:

Oohhh. (*laughs*) That's bad.

PERCY:

No. That's good. The boy grows balls. That's good.

MARK:

Been dying to say that all night, too, Percy. Sorry.

FAITH:

(*to Victor*) Grows balls?

VICTOR:

It's nothing.

FAITH:

Tell me.

VICTOR:

You don't need to know.

MARK:

I didn't mean that, Percy. You don't have to fuck off. (*laughs*) No hard feelings, right? (*laugh*)

FAITH:

(*to Victor*) Tell me about grows balls.

PERCY:

(*to Mark*) No need for any hard feelings.

VICTOR:

It's like he's getting brave.

FAITH:

Balls make you brave?

MARK:

(*to Percy*) The look on your face, man. That's gonna stay with me for a long, long time. (*laughs*)

VICTOR:

(*to Faith*) Sometimes they make you brave and sometimes they make you stupid.

MARK:

Looked like someone pissed in your Corn Flakes, Percy. (*laughs*)

VICTOR:

Oh.

PERCY:

Whoa. This kinda fucking abuse I don't need. (*to Victor*) What you bring this guy here for?

FAITH:

(*to Victor*) Must have lots of balls.

VICTOR:

(*to Faith*) Thank you. (*to Percy*) He wanted to come.

MARK:

(*laughing*) Fuck me. That hurts.

PERCY:

Look at this fucking guy.

VICTOR:

(*to Mark*) Quit that now.

MARK:

(*laughing*) I can't.

VICTOR:

You better try.

MARK:

Not while I'm on a roll, Vic.

VICTOR:

Fuck ya then. You're on your own.

MARK:

Fuck yourself, Vic. Percy, how's your head? (*laughs*)

PERCY:

Okay, laughing boy, you're pushing it. That ain't allowed here.

MARK:

Well, fuck ya then, Percy. (*to Moses*) See how your daddy looks when he's getting shot down? (*laughs*)

PERCY:

> Don't get smart, you drunk fuck. Who the fuck are you to be talking to me like that?

VICTOR:

> Okay. Knock it off you guys.

PERCY:

> Knock it off?

VICTOR:

> Yeah. You're scaring me.

MARK:

> Okay. Okay.

PERCY:

> (*to Mark*) You.

MARK:

> What?

PERCY:

> You're fucking with me.

MARK:

> No. I don't fuck with no one, Percy.

PERCY:

> I'm supposed to believe that?

MARK:

> It's true. Hey, look, everyone's in a good mood, I just thought…

PERCY:

> What? You thought what?

MARK:

> Nothing.

PERCY:

> You thought nothing?

MARK:

Thought we were having fun.

PERCY:

Well, you have a real fucked up idea of fun.

MARK:

(*pause*) Sorry. Have another drink, Percy. (*slight pause*) And shut the fuck up for a while. (*laughs*)

PERCY:

Son of a bitch.

Mark's laughter fades as he and Moses fall to the floor. Mark convulses on the floor in a seizure.

FAITH:

Oh no.

PERCY:

What the fuck is this shit?

VICTOR:

Watch it.

FAITH:

Help him.

VICTOR:

Shit. Can't do nothing for him. He has to ride it out.

PERCY:

Get him up. He has Moses for fuck sake. (*Faith picks up Moses*) Give her to me. Let me see her.

Faith gives Moses to Percy and he goes to the couch.

VICTOR:

(*to himself*) Not taking his medication again. Asshole.

FAITH:

Do something for him.

VICTOR:

He has to come out of it on his own.

FAITH:

Turn him over so he can breathe.

VICTOR:

(*turns Mark over*) What a fucking guy.

PERCY:

What you bring that weak prick here for?

VICTOR:

I don't know.

PERCY:

Don't bring him here no more.

VICTOR:

He can't help the way he is. Fuck, he's harmless.

PERCY:

I don't care if he's Mr. Fucking Dress Up.

VICTOR:

Yeah? How about if he was the Friendly Fucking Giant?

PERCY:

Fuck him. He's a faggot too. Him and that chicken and that fucking giraffe. What the fuck was that giraffe's name?

VICTOR:

Jerome.

PERCY:

Yeah. Fuck 'em. They're all faggots. After tonight you don't bring this fucker back here.

VICTOR:

Snap out of it. The guy's sick.

PERCY:

Tough shit. I don't want him here.

MARK:

Oohh.

VICTOR:

(*to Mark*) You're back. Good.

MARK:

Oohhh… What the fuck was the make of that truck? (*slight pause*) That was a good one. Fuck, that hurts, Vic. Help me up.

VICTOR:

(*helps him up*) You okay now?

MARK:

Never better, Vic. Feel like a million bucks, man. All I need is a little drink to clear my head.

VICTOR:

Take your pills?

MARK:

Fuck no.

VICTOR:

Why not?

MARK:

Don't need 'em, Vic.

VICTOR:

Bullshit.

MARK:

I'm all out anyway. What difference does it make?

VICTOR:

You need them fucking things.

MARK:

Yeah, yeah, yeah.. I'll take 'em when I get 'em.

VICTOR:

Fuck, you're deadly.

MARK:

I know.

VICTOR:

Maybe you should go home.

MARK:

Yeah.

PERCY:

No one leaves.

VICTOR:

What?

PERCY:

You heard me. (*slight pause*) Mark, you realize that you're on the top of my list of people that have to kiss my ass, right?

MARK:

No, I didn't know that. Sounds like a big job though. Why, Percy?

PERCY:

Why? Come sit here.

MARK:

(*sits*) Yeah?

VICTOR:

(*to Percy*) What's happening?

PERCY:

This don't concern you. You and your girlfriend go pick some flowers.

MARK:

Pick me a bunch too, Vic.

VICTOR:

What do you mean this don't concern me?

PERCY:

Just what I said. Me and Mark need a little private time and you're not invited. Simple.

VICTOR:

Alright. (*he goes to Faith*) Ssshhh.

PERCY:

Mark.

MARK:

Percy.

PERCY:

Haven't I been good to you?

MARK:

Yeah.

PERCY:

(*offering Moses*) Take her.

MARK:

Why?

PERCY:

Just hold onto her. (*Mark takes Moses*) What do you see?

MARK:

A turtle?

PERCY:

Look again. Notice anything different about her?

MARK:

(*slight pause*) She seems a lot more relaxed, Percy.

PERCY:

She's dead, asshole.

MARK:

No.

PERCY:

Yeah. Know how she got like that?

MARK:

I don't know. Stress?

PERCY:

You killed her.

MARK:

No. (*drops Moses*)

PERCY

Don't get excited. (*picks up Moses*) Know how long I've had her? She's been with me longer than all my ex-wives put together.

MARK:

Shit.

PERCY:

Now that's a long fucking time, my friend.

MARK:

I'm sorry, Percy. I didn't do it on purpose. It was an accident.

PERCY:

There's no such thing as an accident.

MARK:

Fuck, I'm real sorry to hear that. (*slight pause*) Sorry, Percy.

PERCY:

Don't apologize. A man don't have to apologize for nothing.

MARK:

It wasn't my fault.

PERCY:

That don't matter.

MARK:

I'm sorry.

PERCY:

Stop apologizing. Sorry's not gonna bring her back.

MARK:

What should we do?

PERCY:

No. The question is: What are YOU going to do?

MARK:

Me?

PERCY:

Yeah.

MARK:

Shit, Percy, I don't know. I could give her a little mouth to mouth if it would make you happy.

PERCY:

You poor child. You really don't know when to stop do you?

MARK:

I do.

PERCY:

I do.

MARK:

I do.

PERCY:

Look, we're not getting married here. Listen to my voice. This sound like I'm joking with you?

MARK:

No.

PERCY:

Tell you what, I'm gonna wrap her up with her favourite rock, go outside and give her a good, decent Christian burial. When I get back, you can tell me what you're gonna do for me. Then you can go away.

MARK:

Okay.

PERCY:

Sound good?

MARK:

Yeah.

PERCY:

Okay. In the mean time don't get no ideas about fucking off. I know where you live and I'll come to your house.

MARK:

Alright.

PERCY:

Good boy. (*to Victor*) Hey, Romeo. (*slight pause*) Vicky. Squaw master, I'm talking to you.

VICTOR:

What do you want?

PERCY:

Got a job for you.

VICTOR:

(*to Faith*) Oh boy, I gotta job. (*he goes to Percy*) Yeah?

PERCY:

There's a shoe box on the fridge. Get it for me.

VICTOR:

What for?

PERCY:

Don't ask questions. Just do what I tell you.

VICTOR:

(*to Mark*) What happened?

MARK:

I offed Moses.

VICTOR:

That's what I thought. Shit, that's bad news.

MARK:

No kidding.

PERCY:

(*to Victor*) You still here?

VICTOR:

I'm gone (*to Faith as he exits*) Moses died.

FAITH:

I know.

PERCY:

(*slight pause*) This was bound to happen sooner or later. It's not the worst thing, so don't be too upset. That's my department.

MARK:

You got it, Percy.

Victor comes on with a shoe box.

VICTOR:

This what you want? (*gives him the box*)

PERCY:

That's the kind. (*puts Moses in the box*) Always knew the little fucker would check out before me. (*slight pause*) Well, got some business to take care of. You gonna be here when I get back, Mark?

MARK:

Oh, yeah.

PERCY:

Atta boy.

VICTOR:

What are you doing?

PERCY:

I'm gonna plant her.

VICTOR:

What else.

MARK:

Need a hand, Percy? I could help dig the hole?

PERCY:

No. I gotta do this on my own. (*pause*) Well, I'm gonna get this over with. (*to the three*) Be good, don't sin and stick around.

Percy goes to neutral ground, takes Moses from the box and sets her down. He takes a candle from the box, sets it down and lights it.

MARK:

He's blaming me for this shit, ain't he?

VICTOR:

What did he say?

MARK:

Wasn't my fault, Vic.

VICTOR:

I know.

MARK:

Fuck. I was the one that said we should go party. Shit, we could be at someone else's house right now listening to Ice-T or Gordon Lightfoot and finding out who's screwing who.

VICTOR:

No one forced you to come.

MARK:

I know.

VICTOR:

You got nothing to bitch about then. Worse comes to worse and he wants his pound of flesh, all you can do is bend over and take it like a man. (*laughs – to Faith as she gets up*) Where you going?

MARK:

Fuck that.

FAITH:

Outside. To watch.

VICTOR:

Yeah? Well behave yourself. (*she leaves – watches Percy*)

MARK:

(*slight pause*) Think he's got it in him to forgive and forget, Vic?

VICTOR:

I don't know. He's got an awful long memory. He's still holding grudges from when he was in grade school. (*watching Faith*) But, I wouldn't worry about it too much. Whatever happens happens.

MARK:

(*slight pause*) Think he could kill a guy, Vic?

VICTOR:

I don't know. That's a tough call. But I think maybe he's come too far and struggled too hard not to. (*chuckles*) Don't worry about it. You just have to know how to handle him.

MARK:

That's easy for you to say. You're not the one facing this shit. I been in some ass tighteners before, Vic, but I don't get a good feeling from this one. (*pause*) I'm worried, Vic.

VICTOR:

Well, live and learn. That's all I can say. Live and learn.

MARK:

Oh, living and learning is hard, Vic. Hard. Hard.

PERCY:

(*to Moses*) Live, motherfucker, live.

Pause as Faith attempts to comfort Percy.

VICTOR:

You know it, pal. You know it.

BLACKOUT.

ACT II.

Night. Victor and Mark in Percy's livingroom.

MARK:

I'm losing it, Vic. Swear to God, I'm fucking losing it.

VICTOR:

What the fuck's the matter with you now?

MARK:

I don't like this.

VICTOR:

Neither do I.

MARK:

I'm serious. Must be what it feels like to have a nervous breakdown.

VICTOR:

That's pretty fucking bad.

MARK:

I know. I'm fucked, Vic.

VICTOR:

What?

MARK:

I said, I'm fucked, Vic. I'm so fucked up I can't even think. Sick as a fucking dog too. Wish I didn't drink up all my whiskey. I'm hurting, Vic.

VICTOR:

Better you than me. Suffer, baby, suffer. Now deal the fucking cards.

MARK:

Okay. (*shuffling the cards*) What's taking him so long?

VICTOR:

Couldn't tell you. Low card?

MARK:

It's always low card, Vic.

VICTOR:

Well, today then. Today.

MARK:

Here you go. (*deals Victor and himself a single card*)

VICTOR:

(*looking at the card*) Shit.

MARK:

What you got?

VICTOR:

Seven. What do you have?

MARK:

Nine. Sorry, Vic.

VICTOR:

Do it. (*Mark slaps him across the face*) Son of a bitch.

MARK:

Sorry about that, Vic. Low card gets the ear ringer.

VICTOR:

Just deal the fucking cards.

MARK:

(*shuffling the cards*) Think he might find it in his heart to settle for twenty bucks and a six pack?

VICTOR:

What do you think?

MARK:

I don't know.

VICTOR:

I can't see it happening. Them days are gone for him.

MARK:

That's a crying shame, Vic. (*deals out the cards*)

VICTOR:

Ten. Why?

Faith comes on.

MARK:

Queen of hearts. (*slaps Victor*) Makes things hard on me, Vic.

VICTOR:

That's your problem. Fuck that hurts. I'm gonna remember that.

FAITH:

(*to Victor*) What are you doing?

MARK:

Sorry, Vic. Pain's part of the game.

VICTOR:

(*to Faith*) Playing cards. (*to Mark*) My deal.

FAITH:

You boys play rough. Must be a hard game.

VICTOR:

Not as hard as it looks. Wanna try a few hands?

FAITH:

No.

VICTOR:

Why not? It's a lot of fun. What took you so long?

FAITH:

I was busy.

VICTOR:

I saw. Where's the old man?

FAITH:

Outside. He said he wanted to be alone for a while.

Victor deals Mark and himself a single card.

MARK:

How was he?

FAITH:

He was sad.

VICTOR:

Ten. Come on. Come on.

MARK:

(*to Faith*) Was he mad? Grinding his teeth? Snarling? (*to Victor*) Ace of spades. Sorry, Vic. Just ain't your night.

VICTOR:

Shit.

FAITH:

He was mad, too.

MARK:

You sure?

FAITH:

He's very mad.

MARK:

That's not a good sign. Bring your face here, Vic.

VICTOR:

No. That's enough of that shit.

MARK:

Come on, Vic. I was just getting into it. Don't crap out now.

VICTOR:

No. You had your fun. Time to get serious. (*to Faith*) You want to go?

FAITH:

Where?

VICTOR:

I don't care. Anywhere. Let's just go somewhere and stay there. You and me.

FAITH:

I would like that.

VICTOR:

Let's do it then. Right now.

FAITH:

How?

VICTOR:

How? Well, put your shoes on for once and we'll just get the fuck outta here.

FAITH:

What about your friend and your dad?

VICTOR:

They can't come. They have to stay home.

FAITH:

What if something happens?

VICTOR:

They're great big grown up guys. They can look after themselves.

Percy comes on.

PERCY:

Someone going somewhere? Don't let fear stop you.

VICTOR:

No fucking fear here, man.

PERCY:

You can go.

VICTOR:

No. I'll stay.

PERCY:

Suit yourself.

MARK:

No one's leaving, Percy.

PERCY:

Wonderful. You got something for me, Mark?

MARK:

I been thinking about it, Percy. Thinking about it a lot.

PERCY:

And?

MARK:

And... I can't think of nothing.

PERCY:

That hurts me, Mark.

MARK:

I'm sorry.

PERCY:

(*to Faith*) He look sorry to you?

FAITH:

I think so.

PERCY:

Mark, Mark, Mark, Mark, Mark, Mark. What am I going to do with you?

MARK:

I don't know.

PERCY:

I don't know. Take a look at this here now. (*punches him in the face*)

FAITH:

Oh.

VICTOR:

Jesus. Come on, Percy, settle down. Take it easy.

MARK:

Oh, shit. Ow.

PERCY:

(*to Mark*) Fuck, that must hurt. Don't worry, I know what you're going through. That's happened to me a few times in the past and... I don't want to get into it. (*Mark nods – Faith hands him a napkin*) Yeah. And now you're thinking, what did I ever do to this asshole to deserve this shit. Am I right?

MARK:

You're right, Percy.

PERCY:

I know. You okay?

MARK:

Yeah.

PERCY:

Good.

VICTOR:

I think you hurt him.

PERCY:

No. He's not hurt.

VICTOR:

Look at his nose.

PERCY:

His nose? That's a long way from the heart, Vicky. A long way from the heart.

VICTOR:

I'm not talking about his heart. I'm talking about his nose. Looks like you broke the fucking thing.

PERCY:

(*to Mark*) Is it broke?

MARK:

I don't think so.

PERCY:

(*to Victor*) What did I tell you? I know a broken nose when I see one. Look at that, he's not even bleeding.

VICTOR:

That don't mean nothing.

MARK:

Forget about it, Vic. You got a good punch, Percy.

PERCY:

Thank you.

VICTOR:

Thank you. You guys.

PERCY:

What?

MARK:

What?

VICTOR:

You're both fucked in the head.

MARK:

And you're not?

PERCY:

Yeah.

VICTOR:

No. I'm the sanest one here.

MARK:

Whatever you say. But I'm not gonna take any of this personal, Vic.

VICTOR:

Good for you.

PERCY:

That's what I like to hear. A guy that don't take a slap across the face personal is okay in my books. You surprise the shit outta me, Mark.

MARK:

I try.

PERCY:

Tell you the truth, I didn't expect to find you here. Thought you'd be down in Arizona by now. So, to show you what a nice guy I can be, I'm gonna cut you a little slack. Tell you what, you sing me all the words to Filipino Baby and you don't owe me a fucking thing.

MARK:

Really?

PERCY:

Really. That sound good to you?

MARK:

Sounds good to me, Percy.

PERCY:

(*pause*) Well?

MARK:

What?

PERCY:

Let's hear it.

VICTOR:

Oh, fuck. Dummy up you guys.

MARK:

It's okay, Vic.

PERCY:

Yeah, it's okay, Vic. (*to Mark*) Okay, come on. And a one… and a two… and a…

MARK:

Okay. (*slight pause*) Oh… (*pause – takes a breath and sings*) Oh… Oh my Filipino Baby you're the one. Filipino Baby you're A number one. Filipino Baby you're my queen. Filipino Baby you're my favourite dream. Help me out here, Vic.

VICTOR:

Fuck off.

PERCY:

(*to Mark*) What the fuck is the matter with you? You don't walk into another man's house, kill the only friend he has left and piss all over his best song. I'm not laying down for this fucking shit. (*grabs Mark by the throat*)

MARK:

Okay, okay okay okay. I'm sorry. I'm sorry, Percy.

PERCY:

Fuck that. I been getting that all my life.

MARK:

Hold on. Wait a minute. How about if I give my life to Jesus right here in front of you, Percy? Think that would make you see things different?

PERCY:

You can give your life to whoever the fuck you want after I'm done.

MARK:

TV, Percy, TV. I can get you a TV.

PERCY:

Yeah?

MARK:

Yeah. More than make up for what you lost.

PERCY:

I don't know.

MARK:

Sure you do. Wheel of Fortune. The Urban Peasant. (*to Victor*) Now that fucker can cook. (*to Percy*) Oprah.

PERCY:

Oprah. (*lets Mark go*)

MARK:

Yeah.

PERCY:

(*to Victor*) What do you think?

VICTOR:

I don't know. Take it. Go for it. Why ask me?

PERCY:

(*to Faith*) You?

FAITH:

If you want it.

PERCY:

(*slight pause – to Mark*) I want it. Get it for me. Get it over here. I don't care how you do it, just get it over here.

MARK:

Oh, good. Vic?

VICTOR:

What?

MARK:

That good?

VICTOR:

Yeah, that's good.

MARK:

Okay. We all still friends here? Vic?

VICTOR:

Yeah.

MARK:

That's good. (*slight pause*) Faith?

FAITH:

(*pause*) I think so.

MARK:

That's good, too.(*pause*) Percy?

PERCY:

What?

MARK:

I love you.

PERCY:

Well… that's good.

MARK:

Percy?

PERCY:

Now what?

MARK:

(*slight pause*) I need help.

PERCY:

You're telling me.

MARK:

No. I need help hauling your TV.

PERCY:

No, I don't do that.

MARK:

I can't handle it by myself.

PERCY:

Tough. Not my problem. Vic?

VICTOR:

Don't look at me. I'm not going anywhere.

MARK:

Oh, that's bad, Vic. That's bad. Bad.

VICTOR:

(*to Mark*) Knock it off with that fucking shit now. (*to Percy and Mark*) Both of you. Knock it off. You're driving me up the wall. (*to Percy*) Go with him to get the fucking thing. That's all you have to do.

PERCY:

What?

VICTOR:

You heard me.

PERCY:

Jesus. What a fucking bunch. Okay. (*he exits*)

VICTOR:

(*slight pause*) Better watch your ass, okay?

MARK:

Why?

VICTOR:

Just do it. You're not out of the woods yet.

MARK:

What do you mean?

VICTOR:

Don't trust him.

MARK:

What? Vic, that's your dad you're talking about.

VICTOR:

Don't matter. He could be the Pope for all I care. He can be a mean motherfucker when he wants to be.

MARK:

I know. But everything's okay now, Vic.

VICTOR:

Think so?

MARK:

Yeah.

VICTOR:

Well, think whatever you want. It's up to you.

MARK:

Like... I know you guys for a long time, you know? I know how you are and how Percy is. I know he really don't mean the things he does. Just the way he is.

VICTOR:

Whatever.

MARK:

Okay. Once I square up with him everything will go back to the way it was. You'll see.

VICTOR:

Okay. Sure. Alright. (*to Faith*) You still love me?

FAITH:

(*yawns and stretches*) You know it, Vicky.

VICTOR:

Hmm.

Percy comes on wearing a black coat.

MARK:

Hey, Percy, nice threads, man.

PERCY:

Yeah. Keeps me standing straight and tall. Nothing like a well dressed Aboriginal all groomed and ready for compensation.

VICTOR:

Holy shit. You look like a fucking Hutterite stud, for Christ sake.

PERCY:

Thanks. (*chuckles*)

MARK:

(*to Percy*) You ready?

PERCY:

Just waiting for you.

MARK:

Well, let's head out. (*to Victor and Faith*) Hey, we'll see you Aboriginals later, okay?

VICTOR:

Alright. Walk safely.

MARK:

We will.

PERCY:

(*to Mark as they exit*) What kind of unit we looking at here?

MARK:

Oh hey, it's beautiful unit, Percy.

PERCY:

Better be.

MARK:

It is, believe me. Trust in me. I wouldn't shit you.

Pause.

VICTOR:

Fuck, I thought they'd never shut up and leave. Christ, I don't believe it. They're like women for fuck sake. No, they're worse than women. (*pause*) Sorry.

FAITH:

It's alright.

VICTOR:

I didn't mean that.

FAITH:

I know.

VICTOR:

Don't start that shit again.

FAITH:

What shit?

VICTOR:

You know what I'm talking about. I know this. I know that. That shit.

FAITH:

Okay.

VICTOR:

Fuck, I need something and I don't know what. I never felt this tired before.

FAITH:

I know. Me too.

VICTOR:

Them fucking guys wear me out. Serious. My bones are aching.

FAITH:

Mine too.

VICTOR:

Yeah?

FAITH:

Yeah. Stretch.

VICTOR:

What?

FAITH:

Stretch. Stretch way up to the sky till it hurts.

VICTOR:

Why?

FAITH:

To wake you up. It will wake you up.

VICTOR:

No shit?

FAITH:

No shit. Try it.

VICTOR:

(*stretches*) Yeah, that's good.

FAITH:

Some more. As hard as you can.

VICTOR:

Oh, I can feel it now. Feels like I'm cracking up.

FAITH:

I know. Do you like it?

VICTOR:

Yeah.

FAITH:

Do it all the time. Every chance you get.

VICTOR:

How about in my spare time?

FAITH:

Do you feel better?

VICTOR:

Yeah. Feels great.

FAITH:

Can I rub your neck and make you feel better than that?

VICTOR:

Go right ahead. Rub away.

FAITH:

Okay. (*she massages his neck*) How is it? Right on?

FAITH :

Right on?

VICTOR:

Oh, yeah.

FAITH:(

(*slight pause*) Are you going to live here?

VICTOR:

Here? Yeah.

VICTOR:

I'm thinking about it.

FAITH:

Oh.

VICTOR:

What?

FAITH:

Nothing.

VICTOR:

Tell me.

FAITH:

Never mind.

VICTOR:

No. Tell me.

FAITH:

(*slight pause*) Do you like it here?

VICTOR:

It's alright.

FAITH:

You think so?

VICTOR:

Yeah. Why, what's wrong with it?

FAITH:

It's messy. And that skull of that thing over there…

VICTOR:

It's not real.

FAITH:

(*pause*) It's still messy.

VICTOR:

So?

FAITH:

It's not good for you.

VICTOR:

That right?

FAITH:

Yeah. I stayed in places before that had dirt on the floor.

VICTOR:

That's good.

FAITH:

Yeah. But it was nice dirt.

VICTOR:

There's a difference?

FAITH:

Yeah. Nice dirt feels good.

VICTOR:

That a fact?

FAITH:

That's a fact. There's no nice dirt here.

VICTOR:

No?

FAITH:

No.

VICTOR:

That's too bad.

FAITH:

Yeah. Makes it hard to breathe. (*slight pause*) Do you want me to dance for you?

VICTOR:

What?

FAITH:

I can dance for you if you want me to.

VICTOR:

For sure?

FAITH:

I will.

VICTOR:

When?

FAITH:

Right now.

VICTOR:

Well… if it's no trouble.

FAITH:

It's no trouble. (*stops massaging*)

VICTOR:

Wait a minute. There's no music. We need music.

FAITH:

Make some.

VICTOR:

I'm gonna need something for that. Maybe an empty beer box and some beer caps. You know, something to shake and rattle and bang on.

FAITH:

No. Make some in your head.

VICTOR:

Yeah?

FAITH:

Of course. You'll hear it.

VICTOR:

Yeah?

FAITH:

If you want to hear it you will. (*slight pause*) Are you ready?

VICTOR:

Ready when you are.

FAITH:

Do you hear it?

VICTOR:

What?

FAITH:

Music.

VICTOR:

Oh, yeah. (*slight pause*) Here it comes. Hear it?

FAITH:

No. Does it sound good to you?

VICTOR:

Yeah.

FAITH:

Okay.

Faith dances. Victor lights a cigarette.

VICTOR:

Hmm. (*slight pause*) Wow. Hmm... That's nice. (*pause*) Holy shit.

FAITH:

Do you like it?

VICTOR:

It's alright.

FAITH:

Tell me when you want me to stop.

VICTOR:

Okay. But you're doing good so far.

FAITH:

Are you sure?

VICTOR:

I'm sure. I'd tell you if you weren't. You've done this before, right?

FAITH:

No.

VICTOR:

Don't lie to me.

FAITH:

I'm not. I've never done this for anyone. Only you.

VICTOR:

Don't bullshit me, please.

FAITH:

Okay. Only a few times I've done it before.

VICTOR:

That's what I thought. You're pretty good at it.

FAITH:

Thank you. I've been doing it for a while.

VICTOR:

It shows. You're very talented.

FAITH:

You think so?

VICTOR:

I know so. I know talent when I see it and you're very, very talented. Where does talent like that come from?

FAITH:

I don't know.

VICTOR:

I think you either have it or you don't. Probably you're born with it. Maybe it's like a gift. Like a gift from God or something.

FAITH:

Maybe. (*slight pause*) I would lay with you if I could.

VICTOR:

Okay, stop. Best offer I had all night.

Slight pause.

FAITH:

Right here?

VICTOR:

Why not?

FAITH:

It's crazy.

VICTOR:

I know it's crazy. Nothing wrong with that.

FAITH:

Okay.

VICTOR:

Watch the cup. Don't hurt the cards.

FAITH:

Put your smoke out.

VICTOR:

Right.

FAITH:

Turn the lights out.

VICTOR:

Do I have to? I like to see what I'm doing.

FAITH:

Turn them off.

VICTOR:

Right. Right, right, right.

Pause as Victor turns off the lights.

FAITH:

Can you see?

VICTOR:

No.

FAITH:

Good.

VICTOR:

Where are you?

FAITH:

In the same place.

VICTOR:

Okay. Keep talking so I know where you are.

FAITH:

I don't know what to say.

VICTOR:

Keep going.

FAITH:

(*slight pause*) Where do you do your shopping?

VICTOR:

What?

FAITH:

Did you find any good sales lately?

VICTOR:

No. (*slight pause*) Hi.

FAITH:

Hi.

VICTOR:

How you doing?

FAITH:

Okay. You?

VICTOR:

Not bad.

FAITH:

That's good.

VICTOR:

What's this?

FAITH:

My elbow.

VICTOR:

Oh. Can you put it somewhere else?

FAITH:

Where do you want me to put it?

VICTOR:

Somewhere else.

FAITH:

How's that?

VICTOR:

Better. Give me a hickey.

FAITH:

Why?

VICTOR:

Because I like them. Give me three or four or five even.

FAITH:

Yuck.

VICTOR:

What?

FAITH:

I don't like them.

VICTOR:

Why not?

FAITH:

Because they're ugly and they give you cancer.

VICTOR:

No they don't.

FAITH:

Sure.

VICTOR:

I been getting hickeys since I was twelve and I'm fit as a fiddle.

FAITH:

Oh.

VICTOR:

What?

FAITH:

That's nice.

VICTOR:

You like that?

FAITH:

It gives me some chills.

VICTOR:

That's what I do best.

FAITH:

Oh.

VICTOR:

Yeah.

FAITH:

Oh.

VICTOR:

Yeah.

FAITH:

Oh. You're like an old washing machine.

VICTOR:

Thank you.

FAITH:

You're welcome. Oh.

VICTOR:

Oh.

FAITH:

What's wrong?

VICTOR:

I can't.

FAITH:

Why? What's the matter? Are you worried about your friend?

VICTOR:

No. No, fuck no. I'm cramping up.

FAITH:

Where?

VICTOR:

My arms and one leg.

FAITH:

Walk around and it will go away.

VICTOR:

Yeah. Sorry about that.

FAITH:

That's okay.

VICTOR:

First time that's ever happened.

FAITH:

Don't worry about it. There's a first time for everything. Look after yourself.

VICTOR:

That's a good idea.

Pause as Victor turns on the lights. Faith's sitting on the table lighting a cigarette.

FAITH:

Are you better?

VICTOR:

I'm getting there. What are you doing? Thought you didn't smoke.

FAITH:

I don't. It's for you.

VICTOR:

(*he takes the cigarette*) Thank you.

FAITH:

(*slight pause*) He seems like a very sad man.

VICTOR:

Who does?

FAITH:

Percy. Your dad.

VICTOR:

What makes you say that?

FAITH:

I watch him and see how he is. You should put your pants on.

VICTOR:

What do you mean you watch him?

FAITH:

I watch him do the things he does and how he is to you and everyone.

VICTOR:

How come?

FAITH:

I just do. I watch everything around me.

VICTOR:

Must take up a lot of your time.

FAITH:

He's lonely.

VICTOR:

What do you care if he's lonely or not?

FAITH:

It can kill him. Just like a gun or a knife or some bad tuna.

VICTOR:

What else?

FAITH:

It makes him tell scary stories. (*slight pause*) I can't say any-more. You have to find out for yourself.

VICTOR:

Now what the fuck are you talking about?

FAITH:

I can't say.

VICTOR:

Why not?

FAITH:

It's not up to me. I thought it was, but it's not and I can't say nothing more about it.

VICTOR:

What's not up to you? Be straight with me here now.

FAITH:

I am being straight with you.

VICTOR:

No, you're not. You haven't been straight with me since we met.

FAITH:

Yes I have.

VICTOR:

Well what's all this shit about not telling me what I want to know?

FAITH:

I told you everything I could.

VICTOR:

You haven't told me jack shit.

FAITH:

Maybe I shouldn't be here anymore.

VICTOR:

Why?

FAITH:

Because you're getting mad.

VICTOR:

No I'm not.

FAITH:

You are.

VICTOR:

No, I'm not. (*pause*) I'm not mad. (*pause*) I'm not mad. If I was mad, you'd know it, believe me. So don't say I'm mad when I'm not.

FAITH:

You sound mad.

VICTOR:

I'm not mad.

FAITH:

Something is going to happen here.

VICTOR:

What?

FAITH:

I don't know. But I feel it.

VICTOR:

Are you for real or what?

FAITH:

Of course I'm for real.

VICTOR:

Really? I mean, you're not like some kinda fucking alien or something are you? I'd blow my lunch if you were an alien.

FAITH:

Take my hand. (*he takes her hand*) Does that feel real to you?

VICTOR:

Yeah.

FAITH:

Well?

VICTOR:

What?

FAITH:

Dummy up, Vic.

VICTOR:

(*slight pause*) Know what?

FAITH:

No.

VICTOR:

You never told me where you're from.

FAITH:

I know. So?

VICTOR:

So? So where you from?

FAITH:

Kansas.

VICTOR:

Shit.

FAITH:

That was a joke, Victor.

VICTOR:

I know.

FAITH;

Maybe I'll tell you someday.

VICTOR:

What's wrong with right now?

FAITH:

It's not important right now.

VICTOR:

It is to me.

FAITH:

Why is it important?

VICTOR:

I just want to know. Is that so bad?

FAITH:

No.

VICTOR:

Then why don't you want to tell me.

FAITH:

I told you why.

VICTOR:

Why?

FAITH:

It's not important.

VICTOR:

What's important then if you know so fucking much?

FAITH:

(*slight pause*) Tonight.

VICTOR:

What?

FAITH:

Tonight is important. That's what's important.

VICTOR:

We seem to be having a little problem here. That's not good.

FAITH:

What kind of problem do we have?

VICTOR:

The problem is I don't know what the fuck you're talking about.

FAITH:

That's not such a big problem.

VICTOR:

Maybe not for you. (*chuckles*)

FAITH:

You'll see what I mean.

VICTOR:

You'll see what I mean. What do you mean, you'll see what I mean? Gimme a clue fuck sake.

FAITH:

I can't.

VICTOR:

Come on.

FAITH:

You won't have to wait too long. When it happens you don't have to be afraid. Just let it happen and you will be alright. Everybody will be alright. But you have to stay here. You can't leave no matter what happens. Promise me you won't run away or anything like that.

VICTOR:

I never run from nothing in my life.

FAITH:

Promise me.

VICTOR:

Hey look, I like you a lot. But I don't like the way you're fucking talking.

FAITH:

I know. Promise me.

VICTOR:

What the fuck is this?

FAITH:

Promise.

VICTOR:

Alright.

FAITH:

Say it.

VICTOR:

    I promise.

FAITH:

    What?

VICTOR:

    To stay put.

FAITH:

    Where?

VICTOR:

    Here. I promise to stay here no matter what happens. Fuck. You happy?

FAITH:

    Yeah.

VICTOR:

    Good. Now what?

FAITH:

    Nothing. You can turn the light off again if you want.

VICTOR:

    After all that? You gotta be fucking kidding. Suffer, baby, suffer.

FAITH:

    Okay.

VICTOR:

    Okay. (*chuckles – puts his pants on*) So when this thing happens, what will happen if I decide to like… split?

FAITH:

    Nothing.

VICTOR:

    Nothing?

FAITH:

No. Everything will be the same as it always was.

VICTOR:

Then what's the big fucking deal?

FAITH:

Everything will be the same.

VICTOR:

Like I said, what's the big fucking deal?

FAITH:

Do you like the way things are?

VICTOR:

What things?

FAITH:

(*slight pause*) Things with you. Your friend. (*slight pause*) Your dad. (*slight pause*) Me. (*slight pause*) I'm getting tired of this now.

VICTOR:

Too bad. You're gonna have to put it to me straight. And nice and gently, too, cause I'm not getting it. What about my friend?

FAITH:

He's sick.

VICTOR:

Fuck. You just have to look at him to figure that out.

FAITH:

I don't think he wants to live. You can help him.

VICTOR:

Bullshit. He wants to live. He's scared shitless about dying. Fuck, his voice squeaks when he asks for directions.

FAITH:

What does that have to do with anything?

VICTOR:

What about my dad? I suppose you're gonna tell me he's sick and that I can help him too.

FAITH:

Yeah.

VICTOR:

Well, I gotta tell you, I'm really not into helping people. Shit, I don't know if I'm gonna live long enough to even help myself. (*slight pause*) How do you fit into all this?

FAITH:

It doesn't matter.

VICTOR:

What about me?

FAITH:

You can help yourself.

VICTOR:

How?

FAITH:

By staying here when it happens.

VICTOR:

When what happens?

FAITH:

I can't say.

VICTOR:

Well, fuck, I give up. I can't do nothing about fuck all.

FAITH:

Don't talk like that.

VICTOR:

Like what?

FAITH:

Like about giving up and not doing nothing.

VICTOR:

Don't tell me what to do or how to live.

FAITH:

I'm not. Is that what you think I'm doing?

VICTOR:

What it sounds like to me.

FAITH:

I'm sorry. I won't do that to you again.

VICTOR:

(*slight pause*) That's enough of this shit. I'm fucking beat, man. All I want to do is lay down.

FAITH:

Sounds good to me, Victor.

They go and lay on the couch.

VICTOR:

Fuck man, all I ever wanted was to have a nice life. Get up in the morning and watch the sun come up. Do a few deep knee bends and fuck off to work. Come home and watch the sun go down. You know, live like an Indian.

FAITH:

You can do that.

VICTOR:

Yeah?

FAITH:

(*slight pause*) Yeah.

VICTOR:

Hey.

FAITH:

What?

VICTOR:

You dance good.

FAITH:

Thank you.

Lights dim on Victor and Faith. Mark and Percy come on. Percy pushes a shopping cart with a TV in it. They stop. Pause.

PERCY:

Sure is a beautiful fucking night for something.

MARK:

You got that right, Percy.

PERCY:

Didn't think you had that shit in you, Mark.

MARK:

What shit?

PERCY:

To do what you did. How'd you do it?

MARK:

You calling me a pussy, Percy?

PERCY:

No, no. Fuck no. That's like an insult. I wouldn't do that.

MARK:

Oh, good.

PERCY:

So how'd you do it, fuckhead?

MARK:

Tapped on the door. No one answered, so I let myself in.

PERCY:

Door wasn't locked?

MARK:

Percy, locks are for honest folks. You know that.

PERCY:

Yeah.

MARK:

So, I walked in there and took the fucking thing. Nothing to it. You can do anything once you put your mind to it.

PERCY:

Ain't that the fucking truth.

MARK:

Yeah.

PERCY:

(*slight pause*) I'm telling you, Mark, I don't like the way she's been fucking teasing me.

MARK:

Who you talking about Percy?

PERCY:

What's her name there.

MARK:

Who, Faith?

PERCY:

Who else?

MARK:

No. She's not like that. She wouldn't do something like that. It's all in your head.

PERCY:

Don't fucking tell me what's in my head and what's not. You weren't there.

MARK:

Sorry. Where?

PERCY:

Outside at the house there.

They move on. Faint light on Moses' grave. They stop.

PERCY:

Yeah, fuck, I'm sitting there all fulla grief; she comes up, puts her arms around me and runs her fingers through my hair. Fuck. Thought she was gonna put her tongue in my mouth for fuck sake.

MARK:

No.

PERCY:

Yeah.

MARK:

That's bad.

PERCY:

You fucking know it.

MARK:

What are you going to do about it, Percy?

PERCY:

What the fuck can I do?

MARK:

You can tell Vic.

PERCY:

No. I don't do that shit.

MARK:

He's got a right to know don't he?

PERCY:

No. What he don't know can't hurt him. And don't open your fucking mouth either. Little bitch better fly right or I'll give her what she's looking for.

MARK:

No. You wouldn't.

PERCY:

You don't see no rings on her fingers do you?

MARK:

No.

PERCY:

There you go. (*slight pause*) Come on, let's get the fuck off the street before we end up a couple losers trying to keep track of court dates.

MARK:

Yeah.

They move on.

PERCY:

You did good tonight Mark.

MARK:

Yeah?

PERCY:

Yeah.

MARK:

Oh, good.

PERCY:

Yeah, I'm satisfied. Content. At ease. Shit, I'm almost happy for fuck sake.

MARK:

Oh, good.

PERCY:

Yeah. Fuck, I haven't felt this good since, oh, I don't know. Since I found out I had that extra Y chromosome.

MARK:

Percy's edge.

PERCY:

You know it.

MARK:

Yeah. Vic used to talk about that all the time.

PERCY:

That's my boy.

MARK:

Did all them tests on you and shit.

PERCY:

Yeah. What a fucking sweat box that was, let me tell you.

MARK:

Yeah?

PERCY:

Yeah.

At Moses' grave. They stop.

MARK:

Percy.

PERCY:

Don't say nothing.

MARK:

Okay.

PERCY:

I gotta tell you, this is about the worst pet killing I ever seen.

MARK:

I…

PERCY:

Don't.

MARK:

Okay.

PERCY:

Yeah, worst one I seen was when Abdul Miller strangled his neighbour's St. Bernard for crapping on his patio.

MARK:

Who?

PERCY:

Abdul Miller. Big ol' half Irish half something else guy. Yeah, he choked that big dog and stuffed him in his freezer till it was stiff and set him back on the neighbour's lawn.

MARK:

Holy fuck. Then what happened?

PERCY:

What?

MARK:

Then what happened?

PERCY:

What do you mean, then what happened? Nothing happened. Ab had a shit free patio happily ever after and… we went back-inside and cooked us a big steak and watched the rest of Bonanza.

MARK:

You're kidding?

PERCY:

No. It was the one where Hoss lost his memory and thought he was raised by Indians or some fucking thing. Fucking Hoss. I miss that guy.

MARK:

And the neighbor didn't do nothing?

PERCY:

What the fuck could he do? Ab was the kinda guy you didn't fuck around with.

MARK:

He still around? Wouldn't mind meeting him sometime.

PERCY:

No. He's gone. He fucked up and killed the shit out of a guy. Hung himself in the joint for pills. Imagine that. (*slight pause*) That's the way it goes. One minute you're laughing and scratching and the next you're grease under the wheels of a semi fulla Barbie dolls.

MARK:

Fuck Percy, that's gotta be the greatest story ever told. It's beautiful. Thank you for sharing it with me.

PERCY:

It's alright. (*pause*) Don't mind me and don't get embarrassed, Mark, but I'm gonna go say me a prayer for the dear dead and departed.

MARK:

No, no. Not at all. I'll join you.

A solemn moment at Moses' grave. Mark kneels.

PERCY:

No. I don't do that shit.

MARK:

No?

PERCY:

No. I have very sensitive knees. So get the fuck up.

MARK:

Okay. You're the boss. (*he stands*)

PERCY:

Alright. (*clears his throat*) Our Father…

MARK:

Our Father…

PERCY:

Our Father… who art in heaven…

MARK:

… who art in heaven. This is good, Percy.

PERCY:

What?

MARK:

This is good. Praying is good, Percy. Good.

PERCY:

Yeah, well shut the fuck up then.

MARK:

Okay.

PERCY:

Our Father… who art in heaven… I'm sorry about a lotta the shit I done… in my life…

MARK:

Me too.

PERCY:

Most of the lying and some of the cheating… I'm sorry about it… honest…

MARK:

Yeah. I'm sorry I'm such a fuck up.

PERCY:

… and give us our daily bread…

MARK:

Yeah. Daily bread is good. Good.

PERCY:

… and forgive those who trespass against us…

MARK:

Yeah.

PERCY:

… and I'm sorry about some of the women I banged… and… I'm sorry I can' t stop being horny and what not.

MARK:

Me too.

PERCY:

… and deliver us from evil…

MARK:

Yeah, deliver us from evil. Evil is bad. Bad. Deliver us from evil. Please.

PERCY:

… and look after everyone that can't look after themselves.

MARK:

Oh, good.

PERCY:

And please don't kill my enemies cause I can take care of them with my fucking bare hands if I have to. Thanks.

MARK:

Right on.

PERCY:

Amen.

MARK:

Amen to that, Percy. Amen. (*slight pause*) Hear that?

PERCY:

What?

MARK:

Sounded like a fucking gun shot.

PERCY:

Yeah? Well, better keep your head down. Fuck, I'm hungry. Being good always makes me hungry. You hungry?

MARK:

Not too much, Percy. Not too much.

Faint light remains on Moses' grave. Light on Victor and Faith asleep on the couch. Mark pushes the cart to Percy's front door and struggles with the TV. Percy attempts to help.

MARK:

I got it, Percy. I got it.

PERCY:

Fuck ya then. (*laughs*)

In Percy's front room.

MARK:

Honey, I'm home from the war. (*to Percy*) Where do you want it?

PERCY:

Put it on the table for now. (*he goes to the couch*) Fuck, is that ever cute. If only I had a camera. Mark, you have to see this.

MARK:

(*goes to the couch*) Awww. Shit like that just tears me up.

PERCY:

I know.

MARK:

What should we do with them?

PERCY:

Fuck 'em. Let 'em sleep. They want to waste the best part of the night, that's their problem.

MARK:

No. We have to do something for them.

PERCY:

Like what?

MARK:

I don't know.

PERCY:

Think of something.

MARK:

I'm trying.

PERCY:

Don't hurt yourself.

MARK:

I know.

PERCY:

What?

MARK:

I'll screw them and you can watch.

PERCY:

I don't do that shit. (*chuckles*) You got protection?

MARK:

Always. Always, always, always, always.

PERCY:

You dog.

MARK:

Woof. Bad. That's bad.

VICTOR:

Fucking right that's bad. Prick.

MARK:

Vic, you were sleeping.

VICTOR:

No thanks to you. Asshole.

MARK:

Vic. That any way to be talking to your *compadre*?

PERCY:

What the hell were you guys doing?

VICTOR:

Resting.

PERCY:

That all?

VICTOR:

Yeah.

PERCY:

You sure about that? I'm not gonna find no footprints on my walls or ceiling, am I?

VICTOR:

As if. (*to Mark*) You find what you were after?

MARK:

Of course, Vic. Think we went out into that jungle for fuck all? Come take a look and see what me and your daddy did.

VICTOR:

Do I have to?

MARK:

Only if you want to, Vic. I'm not in the business of forcing people to do things they don't want to.

PERCY:

Come on, get up. I'm not running a fucking flop house here.

VICTOR:

Keep your shorts on. (*to Faith*) You gonna get up?

PERCY:

Let her sleep. She's okay where she is. Let her sleep.

VICTOR:

Alright. (*he gets up and they go to the table*)

MARK:

Feast your eyes on this baby, Vic.

VICTOR:

Hmm. (*slight pause*) Fuck. (*snorts*) You got punched out for this?

MARK:

What's wrong with it?

VICTOR:

Look at the fucking thing. Must be eighty years old.

MARK:

Nothing wrong with that, Vic. Might need an antenna but you can fix that up with a hanger no problem.

PERCY:

Long as I can see the people's lips move, I'm happy. That's all I concerned about right now.

VICTOR:

(*to Percy*) Did you try it out yet?

PERCY:

Don't be stupid.

VICTOR:

Just asking.

PERCY:

Well, don't ask stupid questions. If we tried it out I'd be watching the fucking thing.

VICTOR:

What's eating you?

PERCY:

Nothing. I'm hungry.

VICTOR:

Well don't take it out on me.

PERCY:

I'm not.

VICTOR:

Go eat something if you're hungry.

MARK:

Boys. Boys, boys, boys, boys, boys. There's no need for all this fussing and fighting. There's nothing to fight about.

VICTOR:

No one's fighting anyone, chum.

PERCY:

(*to Mark*) Yeah. Mind your own business.

VICTOR:

(*to Percy*) Leave him alone.

PERCY:

Leave him alone? I didn't do nothing to him. All I said was mind your own fucking business.

MARK:

I'm sorry, Vic. I gotta learn to keep my mouth shut.

PERCY:

I'll tell the fucking world.

VICTOR:

(*to Percy*) Go eat.

PERCY:

When I'm ready.

MARK:

Go find yourself something to eat, Percy, and we'll get this thing ready for a nice night of family viewing.

PERCY:

(*to Victor*) You see? That's all you had to say. What the fuck was so hard about that?

VICTOR:

Nothing.

PERCY:

Right. And now… I'm going. (*he exits*)

MARK:

What's the matter with you guys? I thought everyone would be like… a little happier, you know?

VICTOR:

There's nothing wrong. (*slight pause*) Something's happening here and I don't know what.

MARK:

Yeah?

VICTOR:

Yeah.

MARK:

What?

VICTOR:

I don't know.

MARK:

No? Well save it for a surprise then.

VICTOR:

I can't.

MARK:

Well, what is it?

VICTOR:

I said, I don't know.

MARK:

Is it bad?

VICTOR:

I don't know.

MARK:

Good?

VICTOR:

I don't know.

MARK:

In between?

VICTOR:

I don't know. All I know is something is supposed to happen and I'm not supposed to run away.

MARK:

Sounds bad. Where'd you hear that?

VICTOR:

From Sleeping Beauty over there.

MARK:

Couldn't be all that bad then.

VICTOR:

What makes you say that?

MARK:

I get some good feelings from her, Vic.

VICTOR:

Yeah? What kind of good feelings?

MARK:

Good ones, Vic.

VICTOR:

Tell me about them.

MARK:

What's to tell?

VICTOR:

You tell me.

MARK:

All I can say is I don't see nothing bad about her.

VICTOR:

Well that's good.

MARK:

Yeah. (*slight pause*) Why, is she evil? She's not evil is she?

VICTOR:

I don't know. She's kinda spooky, but I don't know if she's evil.

MARK:

Yeah?

VICTOR:

Yeah.

MARK:

What is it then, Vic? She got some kinda heavy duty mojo happening?

VICTOR:

I don't know. Maybe. I don't know. What difference does it make? Let's just leave it.

MARK:

You don't want to talk it out?

VICTOR:

What's the point?

MARK:

Might do some good.

VICTOR:

Fuck it. Whatever happens happens. Where'd you find that piece of junk?

MARK:

It's not junk, Vic.

VICTOR:

Not exactly state of the art.

MARK:

Maybe not. But I think it saved my teeth.

VICTOR:

I'm happy for you. That's good. So where'd you get it?

MARK:

That would be telling, Vic.

VICTOR:

That's right.

MARK:

Why do you want to know?

VICTOR:

Oh, fuck. Tell me don't tell me. As if I give a shit.

MARK:

Okay, okay, okay, okay. You know Cissy?

VICTOR:

The whore?

MARK:

You know some other Cissy you're not telling me about?

VICTOR:

Not Cissy the whore.

MARK:

Hey, she owed me for a pack of smokes, so I took it out in trade. What's wrong with that?

VICTOR:

She's a guy for fuck sake. And a junkie too.

MARK:

So?

VICTOR:

So?

MARK:

She's human too.

VICTOR:

Barely.

MARK:

Her, I mean, his TV's as good as the next guy's, right? I don't see nothing wrong with that.

VICTOR:

You're one crazy mixed up fucker, pal. You know that?

MARK:

Why?

VICTOR:

Why? I don't know why. You just are. I don't know what the fuck gets into your head sometimes. The old man know where you got it from?

MARK:

Not exactly.

VICTOR:

What does that mean?

MARK:

He thinks I ripped it off.

VICTOR:

That's bad.

MARK:

I asked him to keep six while I went up and got it. Me and Cissy had a little fix, we watched a cockroach crawl across the ceiling and we talked about life. Then I took his TV.

VICTOR:

That's bad, man.

MARK:

I'm hoping you won't tell him, Vic.

VICTOR:

It's my duty to tell him. Sorry, but that's the way it goes.

MARK:

Vic.

VICTOR:

Fuck no. I won't tell him. He'd be crushed and you'd be back where you started.

MARK:

Thank you, Vic.

VICTOR:

Don't mention it. Plug it in. Maybe we can catch the rest of Family Ties or something.

MARK:

Yeah. Or maybe an old Leave it to Beaver. (*he plugs in the TV*) Probably need cable for that. Fuck, I love that show. Remember that show, Vic?

VICTOR:

Never heard of it. There a lot of killing in it?

MARK:

No blood in that one, Vic. Probably gonna take a while to warm up. Wish I had a drink. I'm dry, man. Dry.

VICTOR:

That's too bad.

MARK:

No kidding.

VICTOR:

It's not working, Mark.

MARK:

Don't say that.

VICTOR:

Look for yourself.

MARK:

It was working when I took it.

VICTOR:

It's not working now.

MARK:

Don't do this to me, Vic.

VICTOR:

Do what? I'm not doing nothing to you.

MARK:

Don't even kid about something like that. (*slight pause*) Fuck, it's not working.

VICTOR:

That's what I said.

MARK:

Give it a little kick, Vic.

VICTOR:

Forget it.

MARK:

Maybe just have to loosen up the electrons a bit. (*kicks the TV – slight pause.*) Fuck. Must've been the ride over here that done it. It'll work. (*kicks the TV – slight pause*) Fuck.

VICTOR:

Quiet.

MARK:

Sorry. (*kicks the TV repeatedly – whispers*) Shit. Shit. Fucking thing don't work, I'll hang myself, Vic. Swear to God I will.

VICTOR:

I'll get a rope. Fuck. Relax, man.

MARK:

Relax? Relax? How the fuck am I supposed to relax? Fuck that. I don't have no time to relax.

VICTOR:

Face it, it's fucked, man.

MARK:

You got a screwdriver handy? I'll fix the fucking thing. I'm gonna make this fucking guy happy if it kills me.

VICTOR:

Just leave it. You don't know jack shit about TVs anyway.

MARK:

Thing about me, Vic, is I'm a fast learner when I have to be.

Mark takes out a knife and tinkers with the TV. Percy comes on munching from a bag of potato chips. Mark puts the knife away.

PERCY:

What's all the racket out here? Can't a guy enjoy a decent meal without being interfuckingrupted? Keep it down. Vicky's girl is trying to sleep.

MARK:

Okay.

PERCY:

What are you doing to my TV?

MARK:

Nothing.

PERCY:

Don't look like nothing to me.

MARK:

We're letting it warm up.

PERCY:

Warm up?

MARK:

Yeah. (*slight pause*) Actually, I got some bad news for you, Percy.

PERCY:

Well, give it to me.

MARK:

Maybe you better sit down.

PERCY:

No. I take bad news better standing.

MARK:

The TV's not working.

PERCY:

What?

MARK:

I don't think the TV's gonna work, Percy.

PERCY:

Why not?

MARK:

I don't know.

PERCY:

You don't know?

MARK:

No.

PERCY:

You try turning it on?

MARK:

Of course I did, Percy. Plugged it in. Turned it on. Tried every-thing and it still don't work.

PERCY:

Whose fault would that be now?

MARK:

I don't know. All I can tell you is that it was working when I took it.

PERCY:

That a fact?

MARK:

Absolutely. That don't matter much now does it?

VICTOR:

Fucking thing was a piece of shit anyway.

PERCY:

That don't mean fuck all to me either.

MARK:

Really?

PERCY:

Really. Look into my eyes. These eyes don't bullshit.

MARK:

(*slight pause*) I see what you mean. Fuck Percy, you don't know how that makes me feel.

PERCY:

You're right. How could I? You're you and I'm me. But I'm guessing that you're pretty fucking relieved though, huh?

MARK:

No fucking kidding. Honest to God, Percy, I thought you were gonna fuck me up big time.

PERCY:

That what you thought?

MARK:

Yeah.

PERCY:

You poor child. Nah. Forget about it. I don't do that. Not to a guy that tried. I'm getting way too old for that shit. Gotta leave that rough stuff to you young guys.

MARK:

Oh, good. That good, Vic?

VICTOR:

Whatever. You guys gonna kiss or what?

PERCY:

I'm not gonna go that far. Even if I could, I wouldn't go that far. All I want from you now... from both of you, is to get that piece of crap outta my house.

VICTOR:

What?

PERCY:

You heard me. I don't want it here. I don't wanna see it here no more. Get it out. Take it away.

MARK:

Where to?

PERCY:

I don't give a shit. Far away from here as possible.

MARK:

That's it?

PERCY:

That's it.

MARK:

Come on, Vic, give me a hand. Let's get this fucking thing outta here. We'll take it out back and trash it on the right side of the tracks.

VICTOR:

Oh boy, won't that be fun. Fuck you guys.

MARK:

What?

PERCY:

What?

VICTOR:

> (*slight pause*) Nothing. (*picking up the TV – to Mark*) Well, come on, let's go.

MARK:

> I'm on the case, Vic.

VICTOR:

> Today then. Today.

Victor and Mark exit with the TV. Percy watches them leave. He goes to the table, sits, shuffles the cards and lays them out for a game of solitaire. He starts the game, stops, looks to Faith asleep on the couch. Whistles as he continues the game, stops, drops the cards, goes to the couch and watches Faith.

PERCY:

> (*on the couch*) Hey there, sweet sugar, you smell like chocolate.

FAITH:

> I'm sorry. I didn't think that you would be smelling me. What are you doing?

PERCY:

> Getting close. What does it look like?

FAITH:

> Why?

PERCY:

> Why? Because we make an awful cute couple.

FAITH:

> Yeah?

PERCY:

> Oh, yeah.

FAITH:

> What makes you think I want to?

PERCY:

What?

FAITH:

Lay here with you.

PERCY:

Oh, I been getting the right signals all night long. All night long. All... night... long.

FAITH:

You didn't get no signals from me.

PERCY:

No?

FAITH:

No.

PERCY:

You calling me a liar?

FAITH:

No.

PERCY:

What are you telling me?

FAITH:

I'm telling you that I never gave you any signals.

PERCY:

Really?

FAITH:

It's true.

PERCY:

It's true.

FAITH:

If I did, I didn't mean to.

PERCY:

Think it's a little late to be thinking about that now, don't you?

FAITH:

I don't think so.

PERCY:

I don't think so. Know what I think?

FAITH:

No.

PERCY:

I don't think you know what you're talking about.

FAITH:

You're wrong.

PERCY:

I'm wrong? I'm wrong? I don't think so.

FAITH:

You are.

PERCY:

Close your eyes and tell me I'm wrong.

FAITH:

What?

PERCY:

Close your eyes.

FAITH:

No.

PERCY:

Please don't say no to me. I don't like that.

FAITH:

I said no already. Lots of times.

PERCY:

You did?

FAITH:

You heard me.

PERCY:

I didn't hear nothing.

FAITH:

No?

PERCY:

(*laughs*) Tell you what, you just lay back and let me do all the work. That sound good to you?

FAITH:

No. Why are you doing this to me?

PERCY:

It's my duty.

FAITH:

Do you even like me?

PERCY:

What the fuck does that have to do with anything?

FAITH:

Lots.

PERCY:

Lots.

FAITH:

What is it about me that would make you do this?

PERCY:

You've been on my mind.

FAITH:

You like that?

PERCY:

Oh, yes, I do. I do, I do, I do.

FAITH:

That's all?

PERCY:

That's enough for me.

FAITH:

Do you like my legs?

PERCY:

Yeah.

FAITH:

My breasts?

PERCY:

Oh, yeah.

FAITH:

My ass?

PERCY:

You know it.

FAITH:

My cunt?

PERCY:

We'll have to wait and see.

FAITH:

Do you know what my legs are for? Walking. Do you know what my cunt is for? Pissing. Do you know what my ass is for? Shitting. Do you know what my breasts are for? Feeding my children.

PERCY:

(*slight pause*) You filthy little twat. You just fucked up.

FAITH:

Ow. No.

They struggle. Victor and Mark come on doubling on a bicycle.

MARK:

I sure loved the way them sparks looked flying in the moonlight, Vic.

VICTOR:

You're sure not hard to please, are you?

MARK:

Fuck no. That's what I like about me.

VICTOR:

You and me both, pal. You and me both. (*slight pause*) Good bike.

MARK:

I don't take nothing but the best, Vic. Nothing but the best.

Percy and Faith on the floor. Victor and Mark enter Percy's house.

MARK:

Oh, bad. Bad, bad, bad, bad, bad, bad.

VICTOR:

What the fuck are you doing? What's going on here?

PERCY:

(*gets up – chuckles*) Nothing. Just helping her up. Musta had a bad dream and fell off the couch.

VICTOR:

(*to Faith*) What the fuck are you doing?

FAITH:

He was trying to have some jollies with me while you were gone, Victor.

VICTOR:

Yeah? Don't fucking lie to me. (*he slaps her*) Fucking bitch.

PERCY:

Come on, don't be talking to your woman like that. Nothing happened. She made a little mistake. Big fucking deal. It's allowed. (*he goes to the table*)

FAITH:

It wasn't me.

VICTOR:

Yeah.

FAITH:

No. He come and lay down with me while I was sleeping and said I smelled like chocolate.

VICTOR:

(*to Percy*) That true?

PERCY:

(*playing cards*) What do you think?

VICTOR:

I don't know. You tell me.

PERCY:

She called me over there and said she was having some trouble. Asked me to help, so I did.

VICTOR:

(*to Faith*) That true?

FAITH:

No.

VICTOR:

(*to Percy*) You're full of shit.

PERCY:

Come on now. Don't tell me I'm full of shit.

VICTOR:

You're full of shit.

PERCY:

Don't.

VICTOR:

You're full of shit.

PERCY:

I said don't.

MARK:

Vic.

VICTOR:

(*to Mark*) Shut the fuck up.

MARK:

Alright.

VICTOR:

(*to Percy*) You're full of shit and you're nothing to me now. Fucking zero.

PERCY:

Ouch.

VICTOR:

Ouch.

PERCY:

What?

VICTOR:

What?

PERCY:

Well, what?

VICTOR:

Can't even tell me the fucking truth for once.

PERCY:

(*snorts*) You want the truth?

VICTOR:

Yeah.

PERCY:

The truth is in your pants, boy. And I think you don't have a fucking clue about what to do with it.

VICTOR:

Fuck off.

PERCY:

Whoa. Fuck off? What am I supposed to do now, cry?

VICTOR:

Fuck it. (*to Faith – and Mark*) Let's go.

PERCY:

That all you have to say?

VICTOR:

Yeah. Fuck it.

PERCY:

Yeah, yeah, yeah. That's what I thought. There goes ol' Vicky cruising down the street saying, fuck it. You got no fucking jam, boy.

MARK:

Vic.

VICTOR:

(*to Mark*) I thought I told you to shut the fuck up.

PERCY:

Fuck. Daddy, daddy, gimme a place to stay. I need a place to stay, I need a place to stay daddy. Daddy oh daddy, some asshole ripped off my check and I got no place to put my dick. I hate that cry baby shit. Yeah fuck, guys like you, I screw their fucking wives. Make me fucking sick.

MARK:

Vic.

VICTOR:

Fuck this shit.

PERCY:

Yeah, you were a pussy when you were a kid and you're a pussy now. Faggot. Come here, I'll kick your fucking ass for you. Give you something to fucking cry about.

VICTOR:

Yeah, try that shit with me now. Fucking drop you.

MARK:

He said he was gonna fuck her, Vic.

PERCY:

(*to Mark*) Prick.

VICTOR:

(*to Percy*) Prick.

Victor knocks Percy off his chair.

VICTOR:

Let's get the fuck outta here.

Percy crawls and takes a bat from under the couch. Mark takes out his knife.

PERCY:

(*on his feet with the bat – to Mark*) What you gonna do with that, butter your bread?

MARK:

No.

PERCY:

No. (*chuckles*)

VICTOR:

Fuck.

MARK:

I don't want to do this , Percy.

PERCY:

Do whatever you want. But you stick me with that and I might not die.

MARK:

Oh, bad. I really don't want to… get involved with this…. please…

Mark turns to leave. Percy swings the bat and hits Mark across the back. Mark goes down.

MARK:

… oh my fucking vertebra.

PERCY:

Fucking little rat.

Percy is about to hit Mark and Victor takes the bat away from him. Faith goes under the table.

PERCY:

What the fuck? (*chuckles*)

VICTOR:

Oh, you fucker.

PERCY:

Shit.

MARK:

My back is real sore, Vic. Oh.

Victor stalks Percy with the bat. Percy stumbles and falls. Victor stands over him and raises the bat.

PERCY:

Swing that shit.

FAITH:

No.

PERCY:

Chickenshit fuck.

MARK:

I'm suffering here, Vic. Oh.

Victor lower the bat.

VICTOR:

Fucking asshole. (*kicks him*)

PERCY:

Ouch. You kick like a girl. (*laughs*)

VICTOR:

Fuck you.

FAITH:

Stop!

PERCY:

Oh, Vicky.

Percy laughs, curls on the floor and Victor kicks him.

VICTOR:

That better?

PERCY:

Like a kiss from your girlfriend…

FAITH:

Stop now, Victor.

PERCY:

… and your momma too.

VICTOR:

Don't you say nothing about her.

MARK:

I'm hurt bad, Vic. I think I'm hurt real bad. Oh.

Percy tries to get up and Victor knocks him to the floor.

VICTOR:

I saw what you did. You pissed on her, you bastard. I saw everything you did to her. You think I didn't see? I saw.

PERCY:

What the fuck is wrong with that? (*laughs*)

MARK:

I don't like it here now, Vic. I can't feel nothing. Please, someone, I don't like it.

VICTOR:

Fuck. (*Victor raises the bat – he lowers the bat, goes to the table*) Shit.

MARK:

Vic. Help me, Vic.

VICTOR:

(*slight pause – to himself, in a rage*) You never taught me nothing. (*hits the table*) You never taught me nothing. You never taught me nothing. You never taught me nothing.

He stops, tosses the bat aside and slumps on a chair, exhausted.

PERCY:

Fucking hillbilly caveman.

MARK:

Vic.

VICTOR:

(*slight pause*) Yeah?

MARK:

Mark hurt, Vic. (*slight pause*) Hear me, Vic?

VICTOR:

(*slight pause*) I heard you. (*goes to Mark*)

MARK:

He fucked me up pretty good, Vic.

VICTOR:

Can you move?

MARK:

A little.

VICTOR:

Maybe you should keep still. Might get hurt worse if you move.

MARK:

Think so? Okay. Whatever you say. Fuck, I don't like this. Think I got grounds for a lawsuit, Vic?

VICTOR:

I think so. I don't know. Maybe.

MARK:

Oh, good. I wanna get my lawyer on his ass real bad.

VICTOR:

Yeah, we'll get you your lawyer. Let's get you outta here first.

MARK:

That's all I want, Vic.

Percy finds the bat, goes to Victor and Mark.

VICTOR:

Alright.

MARK:

I don't ever want to do this again.

VICTOR:

I don't blame you.

MARK:

Good.

Percy chokes Victor with the bat.

MARK:

Oh God. You guys are fucking murder.

FAITH:

Noooo!

PERCY:

What the fuck is this shit? (*drops the bat*) What's going on, Vic?

VICTOR:

I don't know. She's freaking out or something.

MARK:

I don't blame her.

PERCY:

Get fucking real.

FAITH:

Oooohh.

PERCY:

Get outta my house. All of you get the fuck outta my house. (*slight pause – to Victor*) Get her outta here.

MARK:

Get me up so I can see, Vic. Vic. Vic, don't let her do that.

PERCY:

Fuck.

MARK:

Jesus, Vic.

Pause.

FAITH:

Hi. (*pause*) No, I'm not scared. (*pause*) I'm a good girl. I am.
I promise and... no, I won't tell. (*pause*) I won't tell and nothing bad will happen to anyone. (*pause*) Okay. It's a secret.
(*pause*) I'm cold. (*pause*) No, it doesn't hurt. (*pause*) No. No.
No. No. (*pause*) Ow. No. No. Oooohhh. Noo.

PERCY:

Fuck off. This is bullshit.

FAITH:

Oooohhh.

PERCY:

Stop. Stop her.

MARK:

No.

VICTOR:

No.

FAITH:

Daaaddy. (*pause*) You hurt me. You hurt me, daddy. You hurt
me. You hurt me.

PERCY:

Shut up. Shut the fuck up. Shut her up.

She screams.

PERCY:

Alright. (*slight pause*) Alright, alright alright. (*pause*) I'm
sorry. I'm fucking sorry. Now get her out. Get her the fuck out.
Out. Leave.

MARK:

That's fucking disgusting.

VICTOR:

You fucking know it. I never seen nothing like that before. You?

MARK:

Never.

VICTOR:

Didn't think nothing like that would ever happen to me.

MARK:

It didn't, Vic. It happened to her.

VICTOR:

I know. But I was here, I saw it happen. Whatever it was, I saw it happen.

MARK:

Me too, Vic.

Victor goes to Faith.

PERCY:

Mark.

MARK:

Yeah?

PERCY:

Get the fuck up off the floor now. I know I didn't hit you that hard. I didn't even step into it. And don't give me no bullshit about being paralyzed with a broken back or vertebrae or whatever the fuck it is you're whining about.

MARK:

Okay. But you're not gonna go ape-shit again, are you? You go ape-shit and I'm laying back down.

PERCY:

Get up and get the fuck out. All of you leave. Hit the fucking road.

VICTOR:

Don't worry about it.

MARK:

Okay. Alright. I'm up. I'm up.

PERCY:

Well, make it fucking snappy.

VICTOR:

(*to Faith*) You okay?

MARK:

What a cranky fucker you are, Percy.

FAITH:

I think so.

PERCY:

Yeah well, live with it.

VICTOR:

Everything back to normal?

FAITH:

Feels like it.

VICTOR:

Yeah.

FAITH:

You stayed.

VICTOR:

Yeah. I didn't want to miss out.

PERCY:

Faith.

FAITH:

(*slight pause*) What?

PERCY:

Put your fucking shoes on. Whatever else you took off, go back to where you come from and shoot your dad.

MARK:

Oh, bad. That's bad. Shooting dads bad.

FAITH:

No. I'd rather let him live with himself.

MARK:

Oh, good.

PERCY:

I didn't say kill him. Just shoot him. Graze him. Give the fucker something to think about.

MARK:

Bad. That's bad.

FAITH:

No. Even that wouldn't do any good for him.

PERCY:

Suit yourself. I was you, I'd knee cap the son of bitch.

FAITH:

You are not me, Percy.

PERCY:

Whatever.

MARK:

Kneecapping good, Vic?

VICTOR:

No. Kneecapping bad.

MARK:

Okay.

FAITH:

I'm sorry if you saw anything bad.

VICTOR:

Forget about it. Nothing I can't handle.

FAITH:

Are you alright?

VICTOR:

I'm okay.

FAITH:

Good. How are you, Mark?

MARK:

A little worse for wear and tear but I'll get by.

FAITH:

That's good. Percy.

PERCY:

Don't ask.

FAITH:

Okay.

VICTOR:

(*to Faith*) Get ready, we're leaving.

FAITH:

Where to?

VICTOR:

Good question. (*slight pause*) Don't matter. We'll find something.

MARK:

(*pause*) Crash at my place Vic.

VICTOR:

Thought you'd never ask. (*slight pause – to Mark*) What?

MARK:

(*slight pause*) She won't take her clothes off like that again will she?

VICTOR:

How should I know? Don't ask me.

FAITH:

I don't think so.

MARK:

Oh good. My mom would shit if she saw something like that.

PERCY:

Vicky. (*slight pause*) Vic. (*slight pause*) What the fuck, am I invisible over here or what?

VICTOR:

What do you want?

PERCY:

Come here and gimme me a kiss.

VICTOR:

Not tonight.

PERCY:

So you're leaving?

VICTOR:

Looks like it.

PERCY:

(*slight pause*) You don't have to.

VICTOR:

I got things to do.

PERCY:

Yeah?

VICTOR:

Yeah.

PERCY:

I guess so.

VICTOR:

Yeah, I guess so.

PERCY:

(*slight pause*) Stick around.

VICTOR:

No.

PERCY:

No? (*slight pause*) Alright.

VICTOR:

Okay.

PERCY:

Well, take it easy.

VICTOR:

I will. (*slight pause*) You too.

PERCY:

What?

VICTOR:

Take it easy.

PERCY:

(*slight pause*) Thanks.

VICTOR:

(*to Faith and Mark*) You guys ready?

FAITH:

I'm ready.

MARK:

(*at the door*) It's been raining, Vic.

VICTOR:

Yeah?

MARK:

Yeah.

VICTOR:

Well, that's good. Rain's good.

FAITH:

Yeah. Rain's good.

Faith and Mark out the door, Victor about to follow.

PERCY:

Hey, Vic.

VICTOR:

Yeah?

PERCY:

See you later.

VICTOR:

Yeah.

PERCY:

Yeah?

VICTOR:

Sure.

PERCY:

Hey, Vic.

VICTOR:

What?

PERCY:

(*slight pause*) You got a couple bucks?

VICTOR:

(*slight pause*) No.

Victor, Faith and Mark outside Percy's house. Percy watches them leave from inside. Mark is studying the bicycle.

MARK:

You want it?

VICTOR:

I don't want the fucking thing.

MARK:

Neither do I. (*to Faith*) You?

FAITH:

No.

MARK:

What should I do with it?

VICTOR:

Leave it if you don't want it.

MARK:

(*slight pause*) Fuck that, I'm taking it.

VICTOR:

Well take it then.

MARK:

Okay.

Mark wheels the bicycle off. Victor and Faith about to exit.

FAITH:

(*pause*) Remember when I told you not to hit me?

VICTOR:

I was wondering when you were going to get around to that. Guess I kinda lost my head there for a minute.

FAITH:

Where was it?

VICTOR:

I don't know. Up my ass, I guess. Did it hurt?

FAITH:

Of course it hurt.

VICTOR:

(*slight pause*) Sorry. (*as Faith exits*) I'm sorry. (*slight pause – snorts – slight pause*) What a fucking guy. (*exits*)

Light dims slightly on Percy's house. Pause, as Percy rolls a smoke and lights it. Pause.

PERCY:

I don't do that shit. (*pause*) Fucking night.

As light fades on Percy's house, faint light remains on Moses' grave.

END OF PLAY.

Hecuba played by Lorena Gale and Raven played by Darrell Guss in October 1994, production of *Age of Iron* at Firehall Arts Centre, Vancouver, BC

photo credit: Paul Michaud

AGE OF IRON

by

Marie Clements

NOTES

Trojan War: A war waged by the Greeks against Troy that lasted ten years. In the ten years, the usually proud and festive Trojans lost much of their passion for their traditions and living ways, having to concentrate instead on fighting an unrelenting war that continued to wage on them. Eventually the long battle subjected them to plagues and seizures that sacrificed them, or forced them into captivity.

The Urban Troy: The urban streets of the inner city where street warriors battle for survival.

Age of Iron:
The blending of Trojan Warriors with the historical reality of the First Nations people of the Americas, the blending of Greek and Native myths, of classical and colloquial languages. Age of Iron – a loss of way for all peoples. An age of war but also of transition, bravery and courage.

CAST OF CHARACTERS

WISEGUY: Veteran Trojan Street Warrior/Elder
CASSANDRA: Trojan Street Warrior/Daughter of Hecuba/A See-er/Prostitute/7th Sister
HECUBA: Trojan Street Warrior/Queen of Mothers
EARTH WOMAN: An earth woman beneath the cement.
RAVEN: Trojan Street Warrior/Half-bird/Half-boy/Half-man/Trickster
EILEEN: Childhood sister of Cassandra
ALFRED: Childhood brother of Cassandra

THE SISTER CHORUS: Three earthly sisters of the streets that eventually join the star consolation of the Pleiades to make the six stars, or sisters in the night sky who watch from above.

THE SYSTEM CHORUS: Detective Agammemnon, a cop (previously a messenger of Troy), a social worker, the watchman, a judge and workers at the mental institution. They are the voices of social, law and governmental bodies which govern the urban Troy.

APOLLO: A Christian priest of a residential school symbolized by the shining God of Light, Apollo, known for his power of healing and light.

THE MUSE CHORUS: Muse Manifestations of Apollo the priest who does his bidding and uses the beautiful choir music of Christianity to manipulate.

ACT I.

The annual re-telling of a legend, a story. Not a new story but one known to all and re-enacted in an Urban Troy Drama. The characters regard this as a custom, a sureness of movement, a festival, a showing off of dance and song, an unfolding of a great drama.

Darkness.

The Planet Mars fades up on the backdrop of the stage. It is pale red and looks to be made of exposed muscles and arteries. It grows redder and more exposed.

Native drumming rises up and as it does it awakens movement from a great breathing city wall. As lights fade up the exterior of the wall is made up of street debris that begins to breath as one and move slightly to the call of the drum. As the living wall awakens the sound of breath increases to form vocals that meet the drumming. As the sound increases the movement on the wall begins to clatter as the wall reveals human shapes of warriors dressed in the iron street armour of shields and masks. Wiseguy emerges from the wall fierce and war-like. As Wiseguy talks, the wall comes alive. Mars begins to fade.

WISEGUY:

The discovery of the first metals and first attempt at civilization thus the earth arose from her confusion. (*SFX: Sound of rain*) Water from her terror, air from the consolidation of her grief, while fire was essential in all these elements as our ignorance lay concealed in these three suffering in the contemporary age, our Age... the Age of Iron.

The stages lights up with different hues of earth. In the centre a red and glowing fire burns.

THE WALL OF TROY:

If I do not understand how the fire came to be, I will burn in it because I will not know my own roots.

WISEGUY:

Ignorance brought about anguish and terror. And the anguish grew like a fog, so that no one was able to see, but a few.

THE WALL OF TROY:

If I do not first understand the water, I will not know anything.

WISEGUY:

So we all lived as if we were sunk in sleep and found ourselves in disturbing dreams. Either there is a place to which we are fleeing; or, without strength, we come from having chased after others; or we are involved in striking blows ourselves; or we are receiving blows, or we have fallen from high places; or we take off into the air, though we do not even have wings.

THE WALL OF TROY:

If I do not understand how the wind that blows came to be, I will run with it.

WISEGUY:

Again sometimes it is as if people were murdering us, though we can not see who or what is killing us; or who or what is pursuing us; or if we ourselves are killing our neighbour, for we have been stained with their blood. When we, who are going through all these things, wake up. We see nothing. We, who were in the midst of these disturbances, see nothing; for we too would seem to be nothings. And you too would seem to be nothings. We have all cast ignorance aside as sleep, leaving its chaotic works behind like a bad dream in the night.

The Wall of Troy begin to disappear in to the wall from where they came.

THE WALL OF TROY:

If I do not understand how the body that I wear came to be, I will perish with it. If I do not understand how I came, I will not understand how I will go, how we will go.

WISEGUY:
This is the way everyone has acted, as though asleep at the time when we were ignorant. And this is the way we must come to a knowledge, as if we had been awakened. (*turns around*) Haaa!...just kidding. (*he laughs and stretches out on the ground and looks up*)

SFX: The rain ceases.
The sky becomes blue and shines with stars that appear one by one as human shadows carrying a white light.

WISEGUY:
Grandmother Moon... I see you and your Seven Sisters... How are you fine ladies tonight? Me? (*gestures to himself*) I am fine thank you for asking... I could be better and I could be worse ... So, yes I am just fine. Wait a minute, where is that Seventh Sister? She's so faint and dim, though it could be these ol' eyes. Don't see like I use to you know, which sometimes is just as well. (*looks up again squinting at the sky*) Let me see here... (*starts to count Star Sisters*) One... two... three... four... five... six. Where are you Seven? Where might that Sister be? Maybe she saw me and thought what a handsome fellow I was and decided to come down and take a closer look. Not likely eh? Well I was quiet a looker when I was younger you know. (*he gets up and starts to look around. Picks up garbage lid and looks in garbage*) Are you in there Sister? So you are hiding on this ol'man... I bet you wouldn't have hid on me when I was a

young man. Geez, I was good lookin' if I don't say so myself. You probably would've taken a fancy to me coming down from the skies. I would've caught you dancing, not at the Number 5 Orange Nightclub or anythin' like that, just kiddin', but somewhere out in the bush where a walker can feel the earth beneath his feet and in him at the same time. I would have seen all you pretty Sisters dancing in secret and I would have just sat and watched, that's all. I wouldn't have scared anybody. Or at least you wouldn't have been scared of me. Nope. You would have looked at this fine red warrior and said, "I'll have to stay here now." That's it. "I'll have to stay here and marry this man." End of story. Except you'd probably miss your Sisters and we'd have to go and visit them once in a while. (*acting like an old woman*) Only problem now is look at me, talking like an ol'woman on her wedding day. Oh well, always a bridesmaid, as they say, never a bride... haha.

SFX: Sound of door opening and music escapes out, footsteps leaving.

MUSIC: "A Tear in my Beer"

Wiseguy listens and then stiffens. The door shuts. Silence. The spell is broken he sits down and stares at the cement beneath his feet.

WISEGUY:

Earth beneath my feet. Poor ol' Mother, suffocating with this heavy load. (*He starts to peel the slabs of cement off the Earth revealing a crust of soil and body like pieces of earth.*) Don't cry. It's okay, Wiseguy's here now. Shhh... it's alright.

Wiseguy's tearing up as many slabs of cement as he can. He hears a rustle behind him. He stops. Rustle. He stops. He puts his head in his hands and pretends to cry. Cassandra is about to talk to him but as of now she is still part of the Wall. The six human Star Sisters disappear.

VOICE:

Why all this crying? This melancholy?

Wiseguy jumps up to catch the Voice. He looks to find the body of the voice.

VOICE:

Have you longed a very long time for your native Troy? With a torturing love?

WISEGUY:

Aye... so that for joy my eyes weep tears upon it.

VOICE:

Then learn that it is a sweet languishing you have taken.

WISEGUY:

(*puzzled*) How so? How do you know? I need a dictionary to master your sayings.

He gets closer and closer to wall. He listens for a breath, reaches in and roughly pulls her out.

WISEGUY:

I should have known it was you my little witch. Cassandra, alright you've got me, how so?

She kisses him affectionately on the cheek and points to the opening of cement. Earth Woman is moving cement off her body.

CASSANDRA:

It is a passion which has stuck inside you and is as passionately returned by her.

Wiseguy runs to Earth Woman and digs his hands in the dirt surrounding her. Earth Woman rubs her earth hands on his face as a caress.

WISEGUY:

(*returning picking off cement from the earth*) A man must speak well of his fortune, though this part is not so good. (*He picks a piece off and throws it toward a open garbage can.*)

FIVE POINTS! (*They laugh. Wiseguy sets in to tell a legend-like story all the time working at the task of tearing the cement off.*)

You have only seen this Land of Troy from the outside. The walls and floors are thick and grim with the wars and plagues and now hardened. But inside it is a beautiful woman, alive with happiness and living. The ancient ones talk to us.

(*to audience*) You envy that. You have no such land because you have covered it with an ungiving surface. You call us bar-barians. But that is what we call you. You attacked our people and keep attacking, because we are truly rich and powerful. And our roots are red from the earth. But most of our treasure is gone. So what do you hope to gain? Glory perhaps? But is it glorious to destroy? Yes, you believe it is. But I am not so stu-pid.

(*gazing up at the stars*) All the lovely things the ancient ones have made and still stay with us, despite ourselves.

(*points upward to each star as they appear*) One sister... two... three... four... five... six. Six Sisters. I would like to meet the seventh one before it is too late.

(*angry and loud, struggles with slabs of cement throwing pieces*)We are civilized, and the wise among us know that we are doomed.

CASSANDRA:
You should be quiet now.

WISEGUY:
Someday, in some way, you will get in, right inside us.

CASSANDRA:
Shhh now.

Cassandra tries to comfort him. She tries to lead him to the earth. Wiseguy sings "Tears in My Beer." He dances wildly and enthusiastically, breaking away from her.

CASSANDRA:

You must rest inside and be quiet. I do not want you discovered.

WISEGUY:

(*following her like a sleepy child*) Yes... yes... I'll let the gleaming wine that has gone down my throat warm me. And I'll talk no more.

He looks at the sky to search for the Seventh Sister one more time and then at Cassandra.

WISEGUY:

I am sorry I am so old.

Cassandra helps him down as the Earth Woman reaches for him protectively.

EARTH WOMAN

Shhh... now. Come inside and try to get some rest. I'll make your bed in my safe corner just as you're used to.

Wiseguy nestles into the earth of the Earth Woman. She holds him in sleep, caressing as a child.

CASSANDRA:

Lie there now beside your roots and when it's time you'll wake.

Cassandra covers them both with the cement pieces so they will not be seen exposed. She awaits. He snores loudly. Both Cassandra and Earth Woman laugh, till they hear the sound of someone approaching.

Silence.

The rattle of a shopping cart and a voice cursing. Cassandra runs for the safety of the Wall. Hecuba rattles her shopping cart on the stage. It is filled with her street treasures and signs which stick out from the cart declaring the end of the world. In the front part of the cart is a doll fashioned in tarnished iron pieces and cast away clothes like it's mother, Hecuba. She fusses with the doll as a mother might with her child. Laboriously, and dramatically she makes her way.

HECUBA:

Old... old legs like sticks. Press on, try hard. Let me bid farewell to my hapless city and all I've got to say is "Good riddance!" Oh Troy, you once held your head so high amongst barbarians. They are burning you piece by piece and leading us out to the land of slavery. Oh ye Gods! Yet why should I call upon the Gods? In the past they did not hear when I called.

She spies the lump of Wiseguy and the Earth woman. She walks over slowly talking back to the child-doll.

HECUBA:

He sees nothing but the city, the great city. It is a city no longer, as the bitch Cassandra says, it has fallen and it can't get up. Troy is dead.

Hecuba is at Wiseguy now and pokes him with her cane till she gets a reaction.

WISEGUY:

Whaaat? What's the matter? What poison have you taken woman. What drug born of the earth or draught from the great water, that you have brought on yourself the fury and loud curses?

Hecuba goes into a rage, she beats him in a spastic manner, hitting the different surfaces for different sound qualities.

HECUBA:

Up... look up... rise from the earth. There is no land anymore.

Wiseguy scrambles up clumsily to get away from her stick. She starts hitting everything in sight, the cement, the ground, the wall itself. When she hits people on the Wall, they comment.

THE WALL OF TROY:
Jeesus... watch what're you're doing? Get the hell away from us. Stupid old bat! Oooaw... ouch... fuuuuuuk... I'm goin'... grr... sqwaaaak! Watch where you put that stick... sqwaaak!

She hits what sound she likes a second or third time, till she gets a strange orchestra of comments, enjoying herself and the sounds. She likes the cry of the Raven's sqwak. She hits him repeatedly at the end, the sound getting louder and louder, until he falls from the Wall with a great thud of protest and a clattering of objects falling from underneath his wings to the floor.

RAVEN:
Sqwaaak... not only did you wake me up but you made me drop my possessions...

Raven picks his treasures up, dusting them off and placing them back inside his wings, indignantly. Hecuba pokes him with her cane.

HECUBA:
I'll tell you who I was and then you'll pity me. I ruled a country once. My husband was king and all my sons were princes. I have seen them lying with whiteman's spears through their hearts, and watched their father die. Now I must be a slave. My dress is torn, ragged and filthy. My whole body's filthy.

RAVEN:
You're not kiddin' me, and stinky and...

Hecuba throws Raven a look of warning.

HECUBA:

It makes me ashamed. And this is Hecuba, who once sat on the throne of the land. What shall I do now? I shall sing and cry like a bird. Aooowww...

RAVEN:

Squaaak.

Both Hecuba and Raven yell loudly, urging each other on into a frenzy of cane hitting and stomping of their feet, culminating into a loud drum like beat.

HECUBA:

When her nest is destroyed and her children.

RAVEN:

Sqwaaakkk.

Hecuba throws her doll-child down and Raven and her stomp on it viciously. Pieces of it scatter and crunch under them.

HECUBA:

I shall sing as I never did when our people sang, when the drums beat.

RAVEN:

Squawkkk.

HECUBA:

... and I was Queen of the Land.

RAVEN:

Squawkkkk.

The voice of Cassandra speaks from the wall in a quiet child-like rhyme.

CASSANDRA:

She will never grow old.

They both freeze to listen. Hecuba runs to child-doll as if it is talking to her. Matter-of-factly she responds to doll and voice as if they are one.

HECUBA:

Wake up... wake up my child. The land is burning. They will be coming to take you too.

Hecuba sits down and tries desperately to put the doll back together talking all the while. Raven picks up the pieces of the doll and hides them under his wings.

HECUBA:

Don't worry... mama will make it okay. Everything will be fine. In a few weeks you can come back and live with me and we will be together again.

Cassandra exits from the Wall and talks softly to Hecuba as she goes to her.

CASSANDRA:

She will always be happy.

HECUBA:

Please don't cry. Be a brave little girl. Momma loves you, momma loves you. You will always be happy.

CASSANDRA:

She will have no cares or troubles.

HECUBA:

You will have no cares or troubles, that's my girl... that's my girl, that's my girl... that's my girl... that's my girl... that's my girl... where's my girl... where's my girl... where's my girl... where's MY GIRL? WHERE'S MY GIRL?????

Hecuba starts sobbing.

CASSANDRA:

> I'm here. Look at me. All the parts together except for the ones no one can see.

HECUBA:

> That's right.

CASSANDRA:

> And Raven's here too. (*to Raven*) Say something nice.

RAVEN:

> Yes... yes. I'm here too, alright. (*picking up a piece of the doll and caressing it*)

HECUBA:

> The crushed skull... forgive me.

RAVEN:

> The Land of Cuckoo Birds!

Wiseguy goes and gets a lunch box, bringing it back to where Hecuba sits.

WISEGUY:

> Oh... oh dear. Here are fresh sorrows, succeeding sorrows still fresh. (*opens lunch box and takes out a first aid kit of strings and glue, wires, etc.*) With bandages, I shall play doctor to its wounds. A sorry doctor, doctor in name with no skill to heal. (*He motions Raven over to act as the nurse.*) Give them to me.

RAVEN:

> What?

WISEGUY:

> The rest of the doll pieces.

RAVEN:

> I gave them to Hecuba.

WISEGUY:

> Now.

Grudgingly Raven passes pieces over to Wiseguy as they attempt to glue, string, hammer the doll together, to no avail.

HECUBA:

Oh arms so sweet to me, like your father's. You hang now loose and lifeless from the sockets.

RAVEN:

I don't think that's going to work.

WISEGUY:

Is that your professional opinion? Who's the doctor here anyways?

RAVEN:

Alright... alright... geez... touchy.

HECUBA:

Oh dear mouth, you are gone, with all your pretty prattle. It was not true, what you used to say to me, climbing on my bed: "Mother, I'll cut off from my hair a great big curl for you and I'll bring crowds of my friends to your grave and give you fond farewells."

CASSANDRA:

You can brush my hair Mother. Here just like you like to... a hundred times.

HECUBA:

That's right. That's right. A hundred strokes before each night's sleep. You're a good girl Cassandra.

RAVEN:

That's the piece there. If you don't put the spring in properly it will look like it has bug eyes. Not that it was a pretty sight anyways, but it will look really creepy with bulging eyes.

WISEGUY:

(*to Raven*) Yeah, well it's not going to look too good with no arms or legs either is it, big feet?

RAVEN:

Fuck it!

WISEGUY:

She's a goner, Hecuba.

HECUBA:

Ah me! It is the other way around, it is I, the old crone, land-
less, childless, who will bury your poor corpse.

CASSANDRA:

It's alright, Hecuba. Raven and I will cut our hair for you when
you die.

RAVEN:

Yah, I'll cut mine bald, if that helps all this.

HECUBA:

Ah, me! All the kisses, all my care.

RAVEN:

(*in mock sympathy*) Ah! You move me. Ah! You touch my
heart. Oh, the mighty one you have lost...

WISEGUY:

Come, let us collect our humble stores. At least we can give a
decent burial to this poor corpse. As Gods have shaped our cir-
cumstances, we cannot aim at splendor... But all I have is yours
to take.

*Wiseguy reaches under Raven's wings and pulls out a beautiful
piece of fabric and gives it ceremoniously to Heceba to wrap the
doll in. Raven gives over grudgingly. Cassandra grabs flowers from
the Wall.*

WISEGUY:

Go then, bury the body in its grave. It has received such ten-
dance as Hell requires. Let it rest now. I imagine it makes little difference to the dead to honour them with a fancy ritual. It
is the living who attach importance to such vanities.

Wiseguy walks Heceba over to the Earth woman. Raven follows amused. Hecuba hands the covered doll to Earth Woman, who reaches up and cradles the child.

EARTH WOMAN:
Shhh... Now come inside and to get some rest. I'll make you a bed right beside me. Just as you're used to.

CASSANDRA:
Goodbye, little sister.

HECUBA:
Oh broken child, the Earth will receive you. Alas... what a bitter sorrow... Oh, my grief!

Wiseguy covers the two with the cement blanket.

RAVEN:
Oh... my grief!

Hecuba gives him an evil look.

HECUBA:
My grief!

RAVEN:
Okay... okay. Your grief. Ah... grief indeed. Ghastly are your afflictions.

Hecuba eyes him.

RAVEN:
Alas... let's sing the Song of the Dead.

Raven starts singing loudly and dances crazily with his wings.

Song: "Swing low, sweet chariot, coming forth to carry me home... Swing low, sweeet chariot...

Wiseguy and Cassandra join in singing. Hecuba runs after them attempting to hit them with her cane as they laugh.

HECUBA:

Strike... strike your head! Strike! Strike! Ah, me! Ah, me.

She starts laughing at them until they can stand no longer and fall on the ground laughing and hugging each other.

WISEGUY:

Oh, dearest woman.

SFX: A police siren is heard, loud and coming closer, red lights swirling, even closer to the alleyway. Wiseguy, Raven and Hecuba freeze.

CASSANDRA:

The chariot will be coming soon to take us.

Three women figures emerge dressed in black and outlined in yellow police chalk. They gather around Cassandra. Three bright stars still remain in the sky sending forth rays of light. Together standing they make seven women... Seven Sisters.

CASSANDRA:

The chariot is coming... coming soon.

The Sisters speak in rounds of chorus.

SISTERS:

To take us back up...
To take us back down...
To places where we were found...

SISTER 1:

... on the ground, face down, squashed by gravity...

SISTER 2:

... Taken out by garbage, and ending there, missing in action, a knife, straight down on the bed...

SISTER 3:

... on the ground, face down, squashed by your gravity, rough hands long flight down, squashed down by your gravity...

EARTH WOMAN:

I am the one you call "Life" and you have made me die in places.

SISTER 1:

I am the one you have pursued, and I am the one you have seized.

SISTER 2:

I am the one whom you have been ashamed of, and you have been shameless to me.

EARTH WOMAN:

I am the one whom you have reflected upon, and you have scorned me. I am unlearned, and you learn from me.

CASSANDRA:

I am the one you have hidden from, and you appear to me. But whenever you hide from yourselves, I myself will appear.

SISTERS:

For we are the pleasant forms which have existed for your numerous male sins, your unrestrained passions in the dark exerted in whispers.

We are your disgraceful and fleeting pleasures found on these streets which have embraced you despite yourselves, while you in turn have silenced us until you have become sober with your deeds and until we have gone up to our resting place.

The fleet is coming.

The three Women figures outlined in yellow police chalk turn to leave. Earth Woman covers herself.

SISTERS:

You will find us there, where we live, and where we will not die again. Where we dwell in peace... the perfect ones. We sit apart from the others. We are the Pleiades.

The three women figures outlined in yellow police chalk disappear as three more stars join the three bright stars in the sky.

SFX: Sound of police siren drawing closer, it stops close by, sound of footsteps, the opening of paddy wagon doors, commotion, doors closing, footsteps drawing nearer.

Cassandra, Hecuba, Raven and Wiseguy freeze as they hear the footsteps approaching them.

COP:

I'm just going to do a check in the alley, I thought I heard some voices.

CASSANDRA:

Run!

The street family begins to scatter and hide.

HECUBA:

God-damned nosy bastards.

RAVEN:

Boost me up!

WISEGUY:

Quiet now.

CASSANDRA:

Shhh.

They all hide in the Wall. The cop walks on with flashlight inspecting area and the Wall. Calls back to his partner.

COP:

Nah, nothing here. I must be hearing things. Can't be too careful.

Quiet.

Cassandra is the first to come out from the hiding place.

CASSANDRA:

I think they would do something bad to us.

HECUBA:

Do not worry about them. I will be here with my cane to bonk them on the head if that's the case. It is all a flashy show of lights and wailing sirens to try and scare the shit out of us. Other times it is not so good but the Wall is always here and you can always hide in the Wall because they cannot see us with their flash burnt eyes.

CASSANDRA:

Can I tell you something?

HECUBA:

When have you ever silenced your tongue? Yes... yes... go on then.

CASSANDRA:

I think I will die like the Sisters.

HECUBA:

I should take this cane and give you a good whack upside the head for talking such foolishness. Do I not have enough to cry about? Do you want to kill me? Here take this stick and just bash my ever loving brains out then, and get it over with.

CASSANDRA:

Okay, okay... crazy bitch. I was just trying to tell you that sometimes I feel like maybe I belong somewhere else.

HECUBA:

Sometimes you're so dramatic.

Hecuba leaves. Cassandra calls after her.

CASSANDRA:

But still it seems everything is so far away here, and so close in my head.

Raven emerges from alley, mocking her.

RAVEN:

I think they will do something bad to us. I think I will die like the Sisters. It is all so far away... crazy bitch.

CASSANDRA:

Are the people kind in their land? I think they would welcome us. If you wash your hair in the rivers, it comes out dusted gold. I always wanted golden hair... imagine golden hair.

Cassandra looks up. Strings of gold come down with a warm golden light. It is web-like and beautiful. She touches it as it touches her body, raising it to the light. Caught in its feel and beauty.

RAVEN:

They'll make us slaves and whores.

CASSANDRA:

Imagine having golden hair. God of the golden bow, and the golden lyre, and the golden hair, and the golden fire. Charioteer of the fires, where... where sleeps the iron. Raven has no song, just one big "squawk."

RAVEN:

Shut up!

CASSANDRA:

When like a blank idiot I put on thy wreath, thy laurel, thy glory, the light of thy story. Or was I a worm, too low crawling, for death? Raven sits on the fence, sits on the fence, feathers ruffled, feathers ruffled.

RAVEN:

I love the night, but now I fear and curse her, to be in one of their jail house beds. Just shut up for a minute!

CASSANDRA:

The Pleiades were up, watching the silent air. The seeds and roots in the Earth were swelling for summer fare. The Ocean, its neighbour, was at its old labour... when who? Who did dare? Why was not I crushed, such a pitiful gem? Squawkk... squawk... some more. Stupid birdman.

RAVEN:

Shut up you bitch! Can't you see what I'm trying to do here? Shut up... Shut up... SHUT UP!

Cassandra quietly talks to the golden web.

Hecuba and Wiseguy come down alleyway.

WISEGUY:

I know where I'd like to go. The SUNRISE. It's a beautiful city. The best...

HECUBA:

What about the FOUR SEASONS?

WISEGUY:

Hooo... A fancy lady tonight, are ya? (*he laughs*)

Music: Instrumental rendition of "Feelings."

Slides project a picture of the lounge of the Four Seasons. A promotional picture, running fountains, rich lounge furniture, a grand piano etc...

Wiseguy holds out his hand to Hecuba.

HECUBA:

Thank you my good man.

WISEGUY:

Think nothing of it.

Wiseguy takes her to the front of the screen. He grandly dusts a place where she can sit. He serves up a bottle of wine. Hecuba fixes her hair coyly, laughing, politely sipping the bottle of wine, swishing it in her mouth and motioning Wiseguy to do the same.

WISEGUY:

Not a bad year for burgundy, if I don't say so myself.

HECUBA:

Quite right... quite right.

RAVEN:

(*Raven sits back sourly watching. His voice dark and menacing.*) I pity anyone that gets sent to the fuckin' Four Seasons!

Music: "Feelings" abruptly stops.

Silence.

Hecuba and Wiseguy stop their play. Wiseguy settles down to spin a down home story. Wiseguy snaps his finger music starts up again.

Music: "Feelings" starts. More grandly and orchestra-like, priming up for Wiseguy's story.

Wiseguy begins to talk in a slow encouraging legend-like manner. Slides appear again in a promotional like manner encouraging the grandness of the story.

WISEGUY:

I once went to the Four Seasons. It was a long time ago. A great house on the foot of Mount Olympus, you know, that high mountain. That was a beautiful place. No one was poor or hungry. It was so warm, so sinfully fertile.

RAVEN:

(*shouting his comments out, as if spitting*) They say it never rains there and the earth has turned to sand.

WISEGUY:

Yes... yes... whatever. And then there's Whistler. The mountains are cool, covered with forests. And down in those plains

below. The grass, or grass... shsss (*he sucks in*). Just kiddin',
the grass grows above your waist.

HECUBA:

Oh, how happy we were in our luxury and wealth. Now what's
happiness? To live from day to day. And if we are lucky...

WISEGUY:

Bingo.

HECUBA:

Bingo? (*she slaps him playfully*) And, if we are lucky, we avoid
being too unhappy as often as we can. Necessity they call it.

*Close to Raven, a screen displays TV static. Distorted pictures of
our society pass by in a frenzy; news clips, evangelists, computers,
starving children, stats, serial killers, Hard Copy-nightmarish
visions.*

Raven hits his head as if to erase images.

RAVEN:

What are you anyway? Slime oozes from your gums (*he gets
closer and closer to screen*). You reek of cesspool. You stink of
despair.

CASSANDRA:

They punish sin. They go with you everywhere.

RAVEN:

They have snakes in their hair!

CASSANDRA:

Why do they exist?

RAVEN:

In the screams of tortured children... in bloodshed and violence... in cruelty and anger... in the stench and the venom of
good things made foul. They drive their victims MAD!

WISEGUY:

That is not certain. No, nothing's for certain.

HECUBA:

Except for one thing.

RAVEN:

What?

HECUBA:

They do punish sin.

Hecuba and Wiseguy kiss Cassandra on the forehead before they leave. Raven begins to dive and peck at Cassandra like a vulture becoming more and more predatory and bird-like and less man.

RAVEN:

She wears a laurel wreath branded to her head, poisonous thorns sticking and pricking a sickness inside her. A good-for-nothing talking narcotic that puts her Johns' to sleep before they've even had time to fuck her. Such a clever priestess... Apollo bred, revealing nothing prophecies of ancient history and the glory of Troy's Song inside, drumming to that different drummer is it? Do you hear me, my twisted blood? Do you hear me?

CASSANDRA:

Shhhh.... the Sisters are coming.

RAVEN:

I don't believe you. I'm no fool. I don't believe a word that spits out of your mouth in fits of epileptic orgasms, or words that sing at me all soft and spent. Isn't that cute? I don't believe you. I don't believe anybody.

CASSANDRA:

The Sisters are coming.

RAVEN:

The Sisters, my feathery ass.

Cassandra is on the floor. Shaking in an epileptic fit. She struggles to speak. Cassandra spits onto her words as a song filters down from her Star Sisters.

SISTERS:

There's a song in the flame	(*weh ya hehy*)
still burning	(*weh ya hey*)
an emerging Troy	(*weh yo hey yo*)
from within and out from	(*oh yo ho hiya*)
the ignorance and fear	(*yo ho hi ya*)
to find the songs left by the trail	(*yo ho hi ya*)
a rekindling of voices	(*yo ho hi ya*)

RAVEN:

I don't believe you... not one word... don't believe you Cassandra. Always got to talk, talk, talk, never letting a guy get half a chance.

CASSANDRA:

The chariot is coming.

RAVEN:

She wears a laurel wreath and her hair runs free and wild. (*he spreads his wings over her*) She'll whirl into a frenzy alright. She knows what it is to come... and come. (*laughs*) No one will believe what she says, because she is cursed in the ol'head. Aren't you Cassandra? Dance in a frenzy for me Cassandra? I never did a bitch when she was having a seizure... Dance Cassandra. Dance. I don't believe you. I don't believe you. I don't believe you Cassandra.

Hands from the Wall reach out and try to help but they can't reach her.

SFX: Sound of footsteps rushing towards them, a police car screeches, a police siren blares. The red light of the siren flashes around Troy. Two police officers rush in, and grab Raven off Cassandra. Cassandra slides down to the ground and rocking herself and mumbling.

RAVEN:

And... I sure as hell don't believe you. Nobody believes her because Apollo cursed her, not me. She whirls into a frenzy. Nothing to see here. Nobody believes her anyway.

The cop takes Raven out struggling with him.

CASSANDRA:

Give yourself now. Let me own you. Please Apollo. I can not. He begged one kiss of me.

Detective goes to Cassandra cautiously talking to her.

DETECTIVE:

Tell me. Come tell me a prophecy.

CASSANDRA:

Will not.

DETECTIVE:

Why not?

CASSANDRA:

Why not? No one believes me. No one.

DETECTIVE:

Then what he says is true. You have been cursed by Apollo.

Detective takes a note pad from his jacket and starts writing after each added piece of information he is given.

CASSANDRA:

Cursed.

DETECTIVE:

But I am your friend. I have been good to you before. Tell me what it's like to know the God Apollo.

Cassandra moves closer to a small light coming from the sky. It is a warm golden light. The sisters emerge behind her in light. The cop follows behind from a distance taking notes. Cassandra walks into the light. It is like the warmth of the sun on her head. She is taken by it and the feel of it.

CASSANDRA:
The sun... I dreamed the sun came alive in my brain.

The light becomes smaller until it fits on her forehead. It takes shape as a cross that gets bigger and bigger to the dimensions of her body.

CASSANDRA:
I felt the light pour into my skull and I knew. (*small light crosses and starts fading in on the stage and audience lined as a graveyard*) I saw a landscape of time spread out before me. My kingdom... and I saw all things to come.

Crosses are everywhere.

DETECTIVE:
Then he said.

SISTERS:
Now pay me. Give yourself now. Let me own you and I will give you time to rule forever.

The light gets brighter and brighter on Cassandra.

CASSANDRA:
I was frightened...

SISTER 1:
I was frightened..

SISTER 2:
I WAS frightened...

SISTER 3:
I WAS FRIGHTENED!

CASSANDRA:
I said...

DETECTIVE:
I said...

CASSANDRA:
I said... I would but I could not.

CASSANDRA & SISTER 1:
My mind was...

SISTERS 2 & 3:
... riddled, scorched...

CASSANDRA & SISTER 1:
... scorched... and riddled...

CASSANDRA:
Scorched!

SISTERS:
With too much seeing.

CASSANDRA:
... and brightness.

Cassandra tries to rub the light off. To hide from it. The Sisters gather around her shielding her from the light with their bodies.

CASSANDRA:
I longed for shadows, caverns, dim forests. All I wanted was to hide from him, from seeing. I hid. I shut my eyes. I wanted so much to be alone in the dark.

The lights on them all fade.

Music: Notes of an organ are played.

With each note the Sisters detach themselves away from the clump taking on a new form. They will put on plastic gloves and become Apollo's Muses.

Light bursts on Cassandra, as the hands of the now Muses touch her. The concentration is on the movement and quality of the hands. A caress, a grasp, a holding, a touching, etc. The feeling that there are too many hands for her to control, and that they are everywhere.

Music: Choir music.

CASSANDRA:
WHITENESS! His heat is white, and despair is white, and madness and the thoughts which race in my skull. Please Apollo, I cannot give you myself. I am frightened.

DETECTIVE:
He said...

MUSES:
So be it. Ah...

Music: Choir music soften.

CASSANDRA:
And he grew quiet and gentle. He begged one kiss of me. I gave my lips to him.

MUSES:
Slut.

DETECTIVE:
And he...

CASSANDRA:
And he SPAT INTO MY MOUTH.

Music: Choir music strengthens.

DETECTIVE:
And he said...

The hands grow more abusive. Holding her mouth, her eyes, her hands. Touching her, molesting her. The Muses word spit out in dark whispers.

MUSES:

Keep my gifts. Keep my brightness in you. See the truth about the wars, and all things to come. But since you have played with me, when you tell that truth it will seem to those you tell it, like toys, babble, babble, and they will laugh at you.

Music: Notes of the organ.

The Muses finish with her and start gathering themselves to leave.

MUSES:

(*laughing, repeating*) So what does truth matter?

DETECTIVE:

This war has been over for some time now. You're ordeals are all over. So what does truth matter? Come, we will take you home. All will be well and we will make you happy.

They exit.

Silence.

Hecuba walks in looking for Raven and Cassandra. Feathers are everywhere.

HECUBA:

What's happened? What's happened? What's happened? Something's happened. Feisty feathers scattered, the smell of it happening. The smell of barrenness. Hers and his. She has been taken by beating black wings.

WISEGUY:

I see the shadow cast over us. Heavy blind bootsteps leave prints to tell the tale. I suppose they have carried them both away from my Native land.

HECUBA:

I suspect the worse. Suspecting the best is for buttered white young thoughts.

HECUBA:

I hear her crying, Wiseguy. I hear Raven crying for what this high flying bird has done. Stop the crying, Wiseguy. Stop it. Maybe it is better to die than live in the sound of nothingness.

WISEGUY:

Enough talk of death here. They have not gone for good. Nothing is gone for good.

HECUBA:

I feel tired, eternally tired, like I could finally lay my head down as if I have stumbled onto darkness and died in the falling. I will lie my cheeks against the cool surface and close my eyes and let all the children I have mothered pass before my mind in smiles, not sobbing violence. Who should I mother now? Who will hear me with child like ears? Who will say, "it is okay, Mother I am here?" Could it be this surface... this hard, hard surface. Nobody could take away this spreading concrete, nobody could lead it, cart it, jail it away. No, maybe this is something I could love for a long time. I could stroke it until it becomes soft with touch and my hands become raw with scraped blood. I could stroke it, that's right... I could stroke it. I could stroke it... That's right, that's right.

WISEGUY:

Hecuba, it will not get soft. It is as hard as it's maker. It will not get soft. Don't hurt yourself. It will not get soft.

COP:

Take hold of her. Will you leave the old woman lying, carrying on? Oh cruel! Lift her up at this instant. Lift her up.

HECUBA:

Leave me old. An unwanted service is no service. Let me lie where I have fallen into darkness. I have cause for falling and lying here. Falling from such a high hopeful height knocks the wind out of you when you land. Knocks the love out of you.

COP:

Hecuba. Hecuba. You know me, I have made many trips to Troy as a messenger. That makes me an acquaintance of yours of long standing. I am here only as a courtesy to tell you the latest news.

HECUBA:

Here it comes...

WISEGUY:

This is what we have been dreading.

COP:

The assignment has been made, if that is your dread. They have been assigned to different masters.

WISEGUY:

Is there good luck ahead for any of Troys' children?

COP:

I can tell you, but you must particularize your questions.

WISEGUY:

Alright then. Who will get poor Cassandra?

COP:

Detective Agamemmnon took her as a special... eh... case.

HECUBA:

What kind of words are these? Just tell me one thing. Did she say anything about the sun... err... Apollo maybe?

COP:

She is in the hands of fate, her troubles are over.

HECUBA:

Her troubles are over. No one's troubles are over until they are over. That's it. I might as well smash my head and tear my cheeks with my nails, nothing will get this sticky sorrow from my skin. She too, is truly gone.

WISEGUY:

Nothing is gone for good. Nothing.

HECUBA:

The masters are everywhere. I am tired of their swarms of words, double tongues twisting things up and down, and down and up, and up and down. The masters are everywhere, I am tired of their big ears, big hands, big mouths. The better to hear you with and leave you nothing. Nothing. That's right. That's right. Echoing the nothing.

COP:

Do not hate me. It is not my choice that I bring you these words.

WISEGUY:

What is it then? I feel you are beginning a song of sorrows.

COP:

They have decided that the bird... How can I speak the words?

WISEGUY:

Just say it.

HECUBA:

Are they bringing him back?

WISEGUY:

Just say it.

COP:

I don't know how to break the sorrowful news gently.

WISEGUY:

Enough! Are they bringing him back?

COP:

They will cage the bird. Now you know the extent of your sorrow.

WISEGUY:

But to hurl him from the battlements of Troy to yet another battle with the irons.

COP:

They will cage the bird now, you know the extent of your sorrow. They will cage the bird now, you know the extent of your sorrow.

HECUBA:

Big mouths...

WISEGUY:

I see the greedy hands of Gods... some men they raise, RAISE from the emptiness to towering heights. I see the hands, your hands... your dirty miserable hands pushing, prodding, pulling us downwards. I see your hands on our back, around our throats, squeezing... squeezing everything for all it's worth, all it's breath, and discarding. Let me see your hands. Let me see your hands and I will tell you the future, Motherfucker. Let me see your hands so I can see your past deeds. LET ME SEE YOUR HANDS!

Wiseguy grabs Cop's hands and unclenches the fingers.

WISEGUY:

Calloused. What do you see Mother?

HECUBA:

Big overworked hands.

WISEGUY:

Working to lead us away like stolen cattle.

Wiseguy pushes him back with each word and finally down.

WISEGUY:

Pushing. (*pushes Cop*) PUSHING.

Wiseguy presses Cop down to his knees.

HECUBA:

Big ears. Do you hear this? You are nothing but a gorgon turning us all into stone.

COP:

Come, come now. Come, come now.

Cop raises his hand and places it over Wiseguy's face, silencing him and pushing him back towards the Wall. Hecuba follows behind raising her cane slowly to strike.

HECUBA:

Pushing. Pushing. Pushing.

Hands from the Wall of Troy reach out and place their hands around Wiseguy and draw him in to safety.

HECUBA:

Turning us all into stone.

Hecuba raises her cane in final assault. Cop turns and grabs it before it connects.

COP:

Come, come now. Let things take their course and you will shown wisdom.

Cop and Hecuba both hold the cane in a show of forces. He slowly pushes her downwards because she will not let go of her cane.

COP:

Come, come now you are powerless, don't think you are strong. There is no help for you anywhere. Just look around. Yourself over-powered. We are quite able to contend with a solitary woman.

Cop grabs the cane and looks at it, he throws it clattering. He looks at Hecuba.

COP:

Come, come now. (*he laughs and exits*)

Hecuba crawls over to it, picks it up and hits things for sound. She mistakenly hits her arm, and starts tapping her body all over.

HECUBA:

That's it. That's it. Doom is on our skin.

EARTH WOMAN:

We used to talk, you and I. Until you constructed a wall and paved a barrier between our worlds. Leaving me here, waiting for the sound of your footsteps on this iced layer. Knowing I would recognize your walking rhythm as a mother knows her childs' sneaky steps. Knowing I would wait, breath suspended, for you to stop your ceaseless greedy stomps over me, destroying everything under your clumsy feet and inevitably everything above.

Gases rising towards your final sleep, child. Walk softly. Wind and water circling around you, child. Sit for a moment in this long time and talk softly. Tell me what you are thinking. Tell me you love me after all theses ages. Show me. Talk to me. I am talking to you with all my powers. I am reaching to you with all my unconditional love. Sit, sit for a moment in this long time and I will make you tea and we can just talk.

Raven is in the dark. He lights a match and the lights dim up on him. He smokes. Enjoying it as much as he enjoys talking. Above him perched on a huge Greek pillar is a large iron bird cage. Surrounding it are other various sizes of bird cages and broken wings suspended. His bird cage comes complete with newspaper lining, a watering trough and a seed dispenser, which when he pushes, falls down in a dish for his consumption.

RAVEN:

The thing is, there is no place to land except there. (*points up*) No little nest. No place to call home. I've been in a few nests when I was young but touched by curious human hands. I've been, how you say, deemed inappropriate for any real nest, for any real length of time. Ousted, boosted, learn to fly, boy! Be a bird! Landing in the air. It's a dizzy flight around, shit flying everywhere. It's a suspended flight, an unwilling flapping, but instinctual, you know, as if I was born to fly.

Raven is lifted from ground towards cage.

RAVEN:

Birds of a feather flock together, ironed in isolation from the rest of the hybrids of the street. (*lands at cage*) There is a pecking order of all the peckers. Looks like I've got my own room with a view. La-te-da. A watering trough for the airborne. (*dips his head in the trough, shakes himself*) Food for flight.

Raven hits the food dispenser. A morsel rolls down, he throws it in the air and catches it in his mouth.

RAVEN:

Better than having to worry about stepping on someone else's crap, which is often down there. Here, it's just my own shit. There's something comfy about that. Honey... I'm home. I say it's like this. We are birds, cock's, vultures, chirpy son of bitches, stool pigeons, pretty little doves, even your cute little pudgy budgie. All different birds in that great cage in the air, know one thing. Down on top of the earth is a heap full of crap, maybe even you, and we have a bird's eye view of it all.

The sound of a bionic Cuckoo Bird coming loudly out of a clock.

SFX: CUCKOO

RAVEN:

Yes, yes I'm doing it. (*shuts the bird cage door*) Don't they know they can't keep the Raven from flying. Stupid asses. Now Cassandra says there not only is no land, there is no place, no real Troy. Get used to it. The howling bitch.

SFX: CUCKOO

Lights flicker as in last call.

RAVEN:

Yes... yes... She says not like before. But there never was a before me. So I ask, before in the Golden Age? Or before she went fuckin' nuts? Maybe there was never a before for her either? Maybe she always was one stunned bird, whore, sqwaking bitch.

SFX: CUCKOO

RAVEN:

FUCK YOU TOO! (*gets ready for bed*) She says the old Troy is inside us growing, waiting for the wakening moment... rising up from the ashes of the earth. Like our dead ancestors are rising up in us, that they're actually in us, like the land is in us. Singing... geez... what a concept. So I'm left here with all these freakin' images. Thanks bitch.

SFX: CUCKOO

Lights flicker last call again.

RAVEN:

Could you just give a bird a minute here? I say whatever they do to her, it serves her right. It serves her fuckin' right! No wonder nobody believes her. Who would believe that huh? (*long pause*) So I fucked her... So I'm fuckin' sorry. I was just lookin for a place to land you know. (*irritated*) Go on then Einstein!

A large cloth is lowered over the bird cage. A spotlight comes up on Hecuba, she is putting a pair of tap shoes on. She will start tapping, trying to get the feel of it, the tap of it. Enjoying the sound at first.

A masked Social Worker, Judge and Cop enter taking authority positions. They will make singular comments, according to their occupations and act as the System Chorus.

HECUBA:

It is all a song and dance. I've danced and sung my voice hoarse until I've been silenced by indifference. You can't hear me, can you? I wonder if you even notice my skin is black. Or is it the first thing you notice and last?

CHORUS:
Dance.

Hecuba tries a dance step. Stops.

HECUBA:
The child climbs up onto my lap. Oh God, the smell of a child's skin. Your own child laying its head close to your heart. And conceived down here in this emptiness out from the darkness... head, arms and hands and legs. A body, a beautiful small body, that fits inside your body, meeting heart to heart.

CHORUS:
Dance.

HECUBA:
If I got an education I would be dangerous. I would consume you, as you've consumed me, chewing me into swallowable bits, which you propel against the cement snuffed and stained. An education allows you to eat.

CHORUS:
Dance.

Hecuba dances. Stops.

HECUBA:
My child's fingers were small movable parts which I would kiss when they searched my mouth for soft words. My child's eyes were round with my wonder.

CHORUS:
Dance.

Hecuba dances. Stops.

HECUBA:

If I had an education... If I had experience. Experience. I have been survivng, but it takes more than that you say, to stack shelves, to do dishes, to iron your shirts, to wait on you, to be your nigger, to serve you lowly, so you think at least someone can look up to you highly. But I did. I did dance because I didn't have an education, just living experience and sometimes that is just enough to eat and love.

CHORUS:

Dance faster.

Hecuba dances faster. Stops.

HECUBA:

It was enough. She would race to me, arms around my waist. Arms around my waist, rooting me to her. Inseparable.

CHORUS:

Dance faster. Faster.

Hecuba dances faster and faster. Stops.

HECUBA:

Her home was in me. Her home is me. And yet with all your education and experience, with all your polite eating manners, you did not realize I was a mother, I could have been your mother, I could of loved you, if only I would have had more money. Money. There is never enough sometimes. She got lost in the dance. I was a mother and now I am nothing. I was a mother and now I am nothing. I was a mother and now I am your FUCKING MOTHER. MAMA will sing and MAMA will dance just as MAMA will fuckin' please.

Hecuba takes off her tap shoes and beats one on the ground to the rhythm of her own song, acappella.

HECUBA:

Dirty fucking mouthy bastards, doom, doom, doom, doom I should rip your fuckin' hearts out doom, doom, doom, doom...

WISEGUY:

Woooo... that's one song.

HECUBA:

Why don't ya give'em a little, "I'm gonna scalp your fucking hair off dance," though it looks like somebody already did that. These people are hairy everywhere but on the head, it don't make sense.

WISEGUY:

Too fertile there I guess. Nothing can grow there. (*laughs*)

HECUBA:

Go on now.

WISEGUY:

Nah, they'd think I was serious.

HECUBA:

So?

WISEGUY:

Only for you.

MUSIC:

Very Hollywood Native war dance stuff.

Wiseguy shouts a great "WOOP" and does a Hollywood war dance. It scares the shit out of the Chorus, they flee.

WISEGUY:

Many wars I have seen both inside my heart and outside. Many wars I have fought both inside my heart and outside. I have seen the land explode with human rage, bombs set in her to get to us two-leggeds, whatever color, whatever race, it is a worldwide circle we have stretched and now has no shape, no reason. The land exploded up to the sky and here and here into me, rocks and iron ammunition, together, tearing its way in and sticking. I know I was land but now I am also iron. I lay there bleeding, looking at the sky, fiery red and simmering mad. Knowing we were all bleeding. Knowing we were all going to survive. I came back half a man, and more and less. Before I left I already was half a man here because of my redness, my race. I thought it would make me whole in their eyes, a whole man. A fighting man has no race, I thought. When I came back half a man and more. I became even less in their eyes. Where to go when you are less and heavy with iron? Troy. It is not so bad. There is an army of us here... of assorted parts, different gaps, shapes, sizes and colours. Still fighting, together we make a whole, an aging and dying whole still weighted by the iron. That was my war. That was their war. That is our war. You can't go home when you're still at war. The younger ones have their own wars that weigh on them, it has its own metal, its own iron-willed fight. All in all. It is in the living, in the surviving. It is in the ability to look down and say, "How are you, Mother today?" (laughs) Me? Just fine, thanks for asking. That is all.

Wiseguy falls to the ground.

HECUBA:
Why don't you put your feet on some real land. (*walks him over to Earth Woman*) Doesn't that feel better? Would you like to dance?

WISEGUY:
I don't know how to tap dance.

HECUBA:
Neither do I.

WISEGUY:
Would you like to dance?

HECUBA:
(*mischievously*) I don't know how to Indian war dance.

WISEGUY:
Neither do I.

They get up to dance. Chorus dancers are about to strangle each other to the ground and disappear in fog that is rising up.

WISEGUY:
We will make our own dance.

They waltz and waltz out.

SFX: Sound of water dripping.

Cassandra rises from the billowing fog. Beneath the fog glimpses of the Sisters moving, hands raising up from the fog, heads peaking, bodies moving.

CASSANDRA:
Where am I?

SISTERS:
(*whispers*) Play the game.

She touches fog as she talks. Words are slow and trying to make sense of themselves. A Social Worker comes in takes a seat and write notes very professionally.

CASSANDRA:
I had a shaking dream... then darkness... a rumbling every-where inside me. I had another dream... it was a dream I had another seizure... it was a seizure then violent darkness, it was only the darkness. (*takes fog and touches it, molds it*) The mice were scurrying at my feet... The swan, white and beautiful, glided into a wolf spitting foam into my mouth like a rabid dog. White foam bubbling up out of me... white foam becom-ing hands, consuming me, directing me, placing me up high and out of reach. Like our dreams were again gutted and left squirming on the streets steaming.

The Star Sisters emerge from the fog.

SISTERS:

I see the course... your course... of course.

SOCIAL WORKER:

Cassandra obviously doesn't want to play the game.

The Sisters dodge back into the fog.

CASSANDRA:

Will not play the game.

SOCIAL WORKER:

A real survivor.

CASSANDRA:

I had the other dream again. A balancing of my brain. I realized over again and each time stronger there are two Troys. Not just the streets, but a first Troy. Unrecognizable from the first is the last. (*pauses*) I have been telling the truth. In the dream I heard the songs of my people. The people of the first Troy. Songs no longer sung, but sung inside to a quiet voice of a child.

Music: The sound of the Star Sisters singing.

CASSANDRA:

In the dreams the song becomes a voice and gets stronger, binding like roots.

The Sisters become a tree trunk, roots extending up and out of Cassandra. Sisters echo certain words.

CASSANDRA:

Interweaving with others, with no songs but one clear voice. Strong but unheard by ears that could not hear them. The dream is quiet isn't it? The voice won't be.

A window of light grabs her attention though the bars. Light streams down on her.

CASSANDRA:

I was taken away again.

SISTERS:

I was taken away.

CASSANDRA:

I woke up somewhere dark again.

SISTERS:

I woke up somewhere dark.

Sisters begin breathing, exhaling painfully.

CASSANDRA:

No place to put me but here... where everyone screams and it is not strange but normal. Strange... and familiar... (*smiles*) They said, I screamed and screamed until the blue and white suits were scattering like muscular cockroaches hiding from the light. I screamed until breathful darkness.

Sisters let out moans and animal sounds with breath and become animal like in body.

CASSANDRA:

Here a lullaby of see-er silence, a watery stillness inside my head. The screams I heard now were a chorus of someone else's bowels. An army of howls, grunts, cries from the under-belly of something larger than myself. And on top of me, and on top of them. They, heaving coarse enraged voices with all their wind for a sound survival. But I was still and caught in a wave, looking for a living peace. A body that did not shake. A mind that did not dream. A see-er that did not seizure. Did not see anything, finally did not see anything but a cool darkness. That was all last night. So many dreams... last night?

The light through the bars gets stronger, filtering the day in.

CASSANDRA:

Light coming in. I knew there was a day. They came quietly in soft hushes, cautious steps. Asking politely, their mothers would be proud. Asking consistently, asking politely. Did he, Raven that is, penetrate me? Penetrate.

SISTERS:

Long and hard...

CASSANDRA:

Rape

SISTERS:

Carnal knowledge.

CASSANDRA:

Take Something about... protruding.

SISTERS:

Long and hard.

CASSANDRA:

Fornicating... willing it.

SISTER:

Asking for it.

CASSANDRA:

Had I been drinking? Had I wanted it?

SISTERS:

Had I been paid for it?

CASSANDRA:

No means no... did I say no?

SISTERS:

No.

CASSANDRA:

A million times I have not said no... But that didn't mean yes.

SOCIAL WORKER:
What does that mean?

Sisters when talking in Social Workers language become quite proper, soft mocking. Letting the words run off their tongues slowly.

SISTERS:
Politely, consistently smooth running liquid language.

CASSANDRA:
What does what mean?

SOCIAL WORKER:
Are you a prostitute?

SISTERS:
(*sweetly*) Who me?

CASSANDRA:
No, I am just sacrificed.

SOCIAL WORKER:
By whom?

SISTERS:
A quick jerk-off. I mean a quick spastic wave in the language.

SOCIAL WORKER:
Are you sacrificed? By Raven?

SISTERS:
Silence suspended.

CASSANDRA:
No, Apollo.

SISTERS:
Silence.

SOCIAL WORKER:
Apollo?

SISTERS:

Eyes that can not see but look each way in me.

SOCIAL WORKER:

Apollo.

CASSANDRA:

A swan in a wolf's costume. Mice everywhere. Foam bubbling, gushing out of his mouth into mine. It was him. IT WAS HIM. Apollo... God of light. Flowing in gowns over top of me... bloated... protruding.

Sisters talk like they are comparing fish or John stories.

SISTERS:

Long and hard.

CASSANDRA:

Penetrating my soul.

SISTERS:

Long and hard.

CASSANDRA:

Extending my seizures.

SISTERS:

Long and hard.

SISTERS:

Ahooo...

Sisters sigh in mock orgasm.

CASSANDRA:

It was supposed to have been a beautiful song. It was supposed to have been a beautiful light. I was supposed to have been a priestess.

SOCIAL WORKER:

You must be tired?

Sisters nod.

CASSANDRA:
  Very.

SOCIAL WORKER:
  Are you dreaming now?

CASSANDRA:
  No the dreams are the truth.

SOCIAL WORKER:
  Shhh... Now. Get some sleep.

SISTERS:
  You go back to sleep!

CASSANDRA:
  Could you turn off the light?

SFX: Click

BLACKOUT.

ACT II.

Cassandra centre stage. Sleeping. Head slumped over her sitting body. Whispers. A pebble hits the stage and hits Cassandra. Then another one and another.

Eileen and Alfred are Cassandra's younger brother and sister. They are dressed as if they've been playing in the bush.

SFX: Sound of water dripping.

EILEEN:
> I dare you.

ALFRED:
> No way, she'll kill me.

EILEEN:
> Chicken... scrawny'ol skinny legs... chicken skin. I should chop your head off and watch your body jerk around the yard, till it plops down and rolls all the way into the river, and...

ALFRED:
> Alright... alright... EEE, you're mean.

EILEEN:
> You'll do it alright. Okay go now. Just put it on her head and run back. She's sleeping so she won't catch yah.

Eileen holds a coarsely made wreath made of branches and twigs out to Alfred.

ALFRED:
> What'll ya give me if I do it?

EILEEN:

I'll give you this if you don't do it!

Holds out her fist to him.

ALFRED:

Eeee... you're ugly.

Eileen pushes Alfred towards the direction of Cassandra. He looks back a few times but his sister is flapping her arms like a chicken. He slowly eases the wreath on her head with satisfaction and is going to make his escape when Cassandra's hand shoots out and grabs him.

CASSANDRA:

Gotch.

ALFRED:

EeeeAhhhhhh...

CASSANDRA:

Stupid fuckin' assholes. Grimy hands. No one's gonna rip me off. Do you hear me? What did you think you were going to do, heh fuck head? I'll tear you f'in throat out.

She wrestles him to the ground. Eileen is squawking like a chicken.

ALFRED:

Don't kill me. It's your brother Alfred. Don't kill me, they made me do it. Don't kill me. It's your brother... remember Alfred. It's me... geez you're hurting me! Let me go!

CASSANDRA:

Alfred?

ALFRED:

Yah, it's me. Holy shit, Cassandra, ya nearly took my head off. As bad as Eileen. Where'd you learn all those dirty words, wow? We were just having fun, you don't have to get so mad or anything.

CASSANDRA:

Sorry, I didn't know it.

ALFRED:

Big grouch.

CASSANDRA

Big stupid.

ALFRED:

Let me up.

CASSANDRA:

Say Uncle.

ALFRED:

No.

CASSANDRA:

Say UNCLE.

ALFRED:

Alright, alright... Uncle. Now let me up.

CASSANDRA:

Say pretty please.

ALFRED:

No, never.

CASSANDRA:

Pretty please with sugar on top.

EILEEN:

Let him up... let him up... let him up.

CASSANDRA:

Shut up Eileen... or I'll...

EILEEN:

Or you'll what?

CASSANDRA:

I'll come over there and chop your head off and let your ol' body jerk around the yard till it plops on the ground doing the jitterbug.

EILEEN:

You heard me! You heard all of us all that time.

CASSANDRA:

Of course.

EILEEN:

You weren't really sleeping were you? You just wanted to trick us.

CASSANDRA:

Maybe.

ALFRED:

Pretty please with sugar on top.

CASSANDRA:

Pretty please with sugar on top... and a blackberry.

ALFRED:

Pretty please with sugar on top and a blackberry.

CASSANDRA:

Why'd ya put this thing on my head?

EILEEN:

It's a story hat.

CASSANDRA:

A story hat. What's it made of?

EILEEN:

Tree stuff. You know, branches and twigs. Alfred and I made it for you, so you could tell us a story.

ALFRED:

Yah, you know, like you use to.

CASSANDRA:

Like I use to... like I use to. Okay sit down. (*they sit crossed-legged in a circle*) Once upon a time, a long time ago there was a beautiful chariot.

ALFRED:

What's a chariot?

CASSANDRA:

It's like a wagon. Like Grampa's has but nicer, it came down from the sun, it came all the way down on the sun's rays. It was a very beautiful chariot that shone and it had many, many very beautiful horses that carried it across the land quickly.

SFX: Sound of horse galloping.

EILEEN:

Who was making it go?

CASSANDRA:

Someone doesn't make it go stupid. Someone goes Yee-haa or something and jerks the reins of the horses and they go faster.

SFX: Sound of horses being yee-haaed. Galloping.

ALFRED:

Who makes it go yee-haa?

CASSANDRA:

Ah, aaa swan. Yeah, a swan.

ALFRED:

A swan?

SFX: Sound of organ notes played note by note throughout story.

CASSANDRA:

A swan. A beautiful white feathered black-billed swan drove

the horses everywhere in the land and stopped to pick up children from every tribe and took them to a big house, far away from here or anywhere.

EILEEN:

I don't want to go anywhere.

ALFRED:

I don't want to leave. Mum and Dad will miss us. I don't want to go. I don't want to go... aaahhhh. What's there?

CASSANDRA:

A big house... and new clothes and you get to learn to read and write and learn about Apollo.

ALFRED:

Apollo?

CASSANDRA:

Apollo.

ALFRED:

I don't want to learn to read and write. What good is it anyway. Can you hunt or fish? Probably not. Can you go down the river? Probably not? And what's an Apollo anyway? Apollo? Weird.

EILEEN:

Ruth went there and she said you can only come home in the summer and that they make you work all the time. And that there are all these ladies dressed in black gowns, and guess what? They're all white. Just these white faces peeking out and nothing else showing. Spooky. And you're not allowed to dance, or sing the songs and you're not allowed to sleep in the same beds as your brother and sisters and you're not allowed to talk to your brothers and you have to pray all the time. Anyways, a lot of nots.

ALFRED:

It sounds dumb. I'm not going there. That's for sure.

EILEEN:
Me either.

CASSANDRA:
I want to go to school. I want to read and write. I want to wear new clothes and learn about Apollo, maybe I'll even be a priestess if I want to.

ALFRED:
It's a stupid story.

EILEEN:
Really dumb.

SFX: Sound of organ notes stop.

They start to get up . Cassandra shoves them.

CASSANDRA:
I'll race yah up to the top of the hill.

They race towards the top of an imaginary hill.

CASSANDRA:
I'm the King of the castle and you're the dirty rascal.

The other two pull her down.

EILEEN:
I'm the King of the castle and you're the dirty rascal.

Cassandra and Alfred pull her down.

ALFRED:
I'm the King...

Cassandra and Elieen pull Alfred down and they wrestle and laugh on the mountain top.

ALFRED:
Look!

SFX: Sound of car travelling on gravel road.

They watch as a car makes its way down a road.

ALFRED:

Run...!

EILEEN:

It's the chariot... Run!

CASSANDRA:

It's just a car. A white car with black wheels, that's all.

Alfred and Eileen run frantically around stage looking for a hiding place. They rest, huddled in the darkness on stage right and left. They start singing a Native song, childlike and softly as if to comfort themselves.

CASSANDRA:

Eileeeeen... Alfred... come back! I promise you it will be alright. Nobody's gonna hurt you. I'll always be with you, I promise we'll be together... I promise. (*Cassandra reaches out towards them*) Eileennn... Alfreeeeddd.

Just as she's about to go towards the children's voices, lights click on. A pure white light defines an area around her in which she freezes. She joins in with the other children's voices, slowly rocking herself.

Three psychiatric workers come in behind her and the light. They are all dressed in white lab coats, they bring in a white transparent screen, a trolley of tools which contains white gloves, a wash cloth, a basin of water, towels, a hairbrush, a toothbrush, neatly folded clothes, a medical wrist band, and a chart to write down what she has on. They set up efficiently, but all the while, watching her. Cassandra starts sniffing the air. Eileen and Alfred have put on their hospital gowns and are still singing.

Eileen stops singing the Native song. Weakly she starts reciting disjointedly, "I've been redeemed, by the blood of the lamb." Red faced and intent to spit words out, she is standing on her bed and stomping up and down on it.

Alfred stops Native song and starts reciting Hail Marys. He's kneeling and frantically praying by his bed as if he has a tick on him. The three workers have finished setting up behind Cassandra, they turn and face their bodies towards her almost military.

SFX: Notes of organ.

With each organ note they will take a step.

Lights fade up on the two patients as Cassandra's light fades down. Cassandra moves from her spot when it darkens and when she hears deranged music-box music. She runs back and forth between the two beds and the patients. The patients respond to her as if they are holding a conversation with her. Their task is very important to them. The three workers change directions accordingly, very systematic, slow and concise. They take out a flashlight and point in the direction of Cassandra as if following her and gradually gaining ground.

Cassandra stops and sniffs in darkness.

CASSANDRA:
Shhhh... the watchman.

She runs to Alfred.

ALFRED:
I'm hungry.

CASSANDRA:
In the snow... they found Sophie and Gertude. Where? Stiff dead.

ALFRED:
You know everything.

Cassandra runs to Eileen.

CASSANDRA:
   My stomach hurts.

EILEEN:
   Tell me a story.

CASSANDRA:
   Long boat ride home.

EILEEN:
   I didn't know.

Cassandra goes to Alfred.

CASSANDRA:
   I'm sorry.

ALFRED:
   Take me home, you promised we'd be together.

CASSANDRA:
   Don't sing.

ALFRED:
   Run away.

She goes to leave and stops when he speaks again.

ALFRED:
   I wonder how nuns pee?

She laughs and shrugs.

CASSANDRA:
   They'll hear you.

EILEEN:
   My head hurts.

CASSANDRA:

Footsteps coming.

EILEEN:

Why?

CASSANDRA:

A light.

Cassandra goes to Alfred.

ALFRED:

I'm hungry.

CASSANDRA:

Don't let him get close to you. Don't let him touch you. Do you hear me?

ALFRED:

Take me home. You promised we'd always be together.

CASSANDRA:

Why'd you pee your bed?

Cassandra goes to Eileen.

CASSANDRA:

Don't talk to him.

EILEEN:

My head hurts.

CASSANDRA:

(*she looks around*) Apollo?

EILEEN:

Don't step on a crack, you'll break your mother's back.

CASSANDRA:

Footsteps.

EILEEN:

I dare you to go get some apples and pears in the kitchen.

Cassandra goes to Alfred.

ALFRED:

You can't hide.

CASSANDRA:

I'm sorry. Apollo?

ALFRED:

A light.

CASSANDRA:

Sh... here comes the watchman.

CASSANDRA:

No dancing.

ALFRED:

Under the covers there's hands.

EILEEN:

They're so fat, no wonder they have to wear gowns.

CASSANDRA:

My head hurts.

EILEEN:

Do you think they have hair under their habit?

CASSANDRA:

Long boat ride home.

EILEEN:

Stiff dead in the snow.

CASSANDRA:

They found Sophie and Gertude. Where?

EILEEN:

Run Away!

CASSANDRA:

Don't sing!

The three workers are approaching closer to Alfred. He gets in bed, draws covers as if he is sleeping.

WORKERS:

Must be the devil's work.

ALFRED:

I'm hungry.

Workers touch his eyes as if to close them, they reach over and pull the covers over his head as if he is dead. It silences him, but loud breathing can be heard. It stops and the breathing transfers to the three workers.Workers slowly approach Eileen and Cassandra.

CASSANDRA:

Footsteps!

EILEEN:

My stomach hurts.

CASSANDRA:

They'll hear you.

Cassandra backs up and watches in horror as the workers are at Eileen.

EILEEN:

Tell me a story.

They motion for her to get in the bed. She does. They place their hands over her eyes to shut them. They draw the cover over her head as if she is dead.

WORKERS:
You can't hide.

Eileen breathes loudly until she stops and breathing transforms into the three Workers whose breathing is now the loudest as they approach Cassandra. Lights on the two beds fade.

CASSANDRA:
No... no...

The spirits of Alfred and Eileen get up from out of their beds. They take their gowns off, and with their pillows make a dummy, drawing the covers over the dummy.

CASSANDRA:
Eileen... Alfred... I'm sorry... I'm sorry...

EILEEN:
I'll race you.

Eileen and Alfred start to run to the top of their hill, they look back at Cassandra. She is walking towards them but just as she starts to bolt, blinding white lights shoot up and blind her.

CASSANDRA:
A light.

The three workers grab her. She tries to run towards her brother and sister. The light on them begins to fade. As their voices...

EILEEN:
I'm the King of the castle... and you're the...

ALFRED:
(*laughing*) I'm the King of the castle... and you're the...

CASSANDRA:
A light. Apollo! Let me go... Let me Go! (*She falls to the ground.*)

The following is a dance of the tasks with Cassandra as the dancer. She is rag-dollish in body as she tries to physically fight them off. Trance-like talking with a vengence, clarifying her own thoughts.

The workers move with utmost efficiency, in their work. They take her clothes off, wash her, search her for lice, brush her hair, tie it back, dress her with new clothing – a white hospital gown. They do this as they talk amongst each other and as if she doesn't exist. They handle her roughly while writing down her belongings and placeing them in a plastic bag.

SFX: Choir music starts up in background as they pick her up and place her in a chair. They circle her, touching her. Cassandra searches for Apollo.

CASSANDRA:
(*hears music*) Apollo? I smell you. I can taste you, you bastard.

WORKER 2:
Dirty... dirty... dirty.

CASSANDRA:
Apollo? Apollo. Answer me. Where have you brought me? Answer me, you piece of shit.

WORKER 1:
I pity her and I will not be angry.

CASSANDRA:
Not again. And again and again.

WORKER 1:
Come on, poor wretched girl. You must come with me now. Accept, give way. There is no choice.

CASSANDRA:
Apollo... Oh Apollo you bastard!

WORKER 2:
Dirty... dirty... dirty.

WORKER 3:

She is in a trance. She must know what is to come. Atonement for her...

WORKER 2:

Dirty... dirty... dirty.

WORKER 3:

... ways.

CASSANDRA:

My God, MY GOD hates this place, much murder, guilt... blood. I can even smell it here. It is a nightmare brought on by the restless sleep of us all. A wet dream, if you can imagine Apollo, inviting, but never delivering, never giving, but gorging in and out like a castrated bull. No fertility just a pumping repetition. Forever humping. You're forever pushing the power inside me out. Till I am taken with no hope of life, giving with no hope of living life.

The workers back away from her, conspire, then return.

WORKER 3:

We know what the bitch is after. The bitch smells old blood and then some.

WORKER 2:

Dirty... dirty... dirty.

CASSANDRA:

Get your fucking hands off me! (*talks to them*) This is a living dream that's caught in a web of golden illusions. I live in terror and confusion, instability, doubt, and division. Yet I am not so divided. I see you, and you, and you. I see indescribable depths. I see those dressed in their fineries, drunk with power and wealth bumping into concrete walls of towers moulded to keep their own excrement in. Pile it all high!

WORKER 1:

What do you make of this?

WORKER 2:

Dirty... dirty... dirty.

CASSANDRA:

I should rub your nose in it. In punishment, like a dog sniffing its own dung. I should rub YOUR... dirty dirty dirty nose in it. (*quiet*) If you are with me in this I can not, can I? In all your fineries you are with me. And some of you may be able to read the sad face of the earth and sky, but you do not recognize the one that is before you, because you do not recognize yourself yet. Maybe I am you. And you are me. I know you are in pain too, bleeding from your own tearing force, your own self fuck. I have found the beginning of the power that is truth.

WORKER 3:

Riddles, that is all.

WORKER 2:

Dirty... dirty... dirty.

CASSANDRA:

See, a little drop of water makes us all clean does it? Then do it. (*she laughs*)

SFX: Sound of a drum beat.

Workers re-dress her, taking off her asylum clothes, and putting on prostitute street clothes.

WORKER 1:

What are you calling up?

WORKER 3:

I can smell the evil in all that she says, like the God-damned stench of the streets.

WORKER 2:

Dirty... dirty... dirty.

CASSANDRA:

Why Apollo, why did you bring me here? Am I finally going to die and share in their death. All their deaths?

WORKER 1:

Where does all this come from? All this violence? All this passion?

CASSANDRA:

It is no great mystery but a truth veiled in darkness, a hand across the mouth, a smell inside so evil and foul I have vomited over myself continuously.

WORKER 2:

Dirty... dirty... dirty.

CASSANDRA:

Instead of hearing my own voice, my own song, that comes to me in quaking dreams, shaking my lips to remember.

WORKER 3:

Just words, that is all... just words.

CASSANDRA:

Let it blow like the wind blows now, everywhere in a storm. Guilt for things done. Guilt, I can smell it on you.

WORKER 2:

Dirty... dirty... dirty.

WORKER 1:

What are you trying to tell us?

CASSANDRA:

I can hear a choir, too. I bet you can't? A choir singing. Can you hear? Not my choir but Apollo's. Not my song. But it stays inside my head... that will never wash away.

WORKERS:

Dirty... dirty... dirty.

CASSANDRA:

It makes the voices drunk with the blood of the Earth. It makes the voices convulse inside my body from the violation of the natural order. They are all here inside me. You have everything to fear. They can drive you mad. Voices revelling and wailing in this house of blindness of the soul. Am I right? Tell me. I know the history of the foulness in this house.

WORKERS:

Cleanliness is next to Godliness.

A gold fiery web floats from the sky.

CASSANDRA:

I am living history. So far. Do you believe me? Do you believe me? Do you believe me, do you believe me?

She wonders over to the golden strings falling from the sky. She touches it, it flows over her, binding around her neck.

SFX: Sound of death rattle.

SFX: Sound of ocean, of water lapping rhythmic.

Lights murky blue and deep.

Raven sits, perched and flightless, plucking his feathers out painfully. Wiseguy is sitting by the Earth, slowly talking. They are separated and not conscious of each other. Lights will go up on each of them dimly, as they speak and then fade. They continue each of their tasks.

RAVEN:

God-damned useless feathers. Smell of flight sticking to me. Smell of some mangy old shit hawk of a bird. I'll pluck myself. I'll pluck myself. I'll pluck myself 'till... 'till... God-dammit anyways!

WISEGUY:

Death came to her at midnight. I can feel it. She was arranging her hair, binding it up in ribbons for the night, and a golden mirror's endless sunlight held her gaze upwards. Always upwards with that girl. The ribbons began binding around her neck and pulling up while her mind and body pulled downwards with their weight. Weight of war. She is somewhere between the soil of Troy and the dances of the Stars. I can feel it.

SFX: The voices of the Judge, Social Worker and Cop in whispered audio, as if filtered through water.

Cassandra sits on another part of the stage. Spotlight on her as Muses turn in and circle in repetition.

SOCIAL WORKER/JUDGE/COP:
So what does truth matter?

MUSES:
AGAIN.

JUDGE:
So what does truth matter?

CASSANDRA:
Apollo, God of talking hands taught me first.

SOCIAL WORKER:
So what does truth matter?

MUSES:
They say he wanted you the first time he laid his han... eyes on you. Although a God, a man of cloth, though of questionable textures.

COP:
So what does truth matter?

MUSE:
Was he in love with you? Not in a biblical sense, God forbid, but I mean, did he have an affection for you. Surely it must have been an innocent concern for a child... A...

JUDGE:

So what does truth matter?

CASSANDRA:

He wrestled with me, if you know what I mean, God forbid. And his breath was warm and moving moist.

MUSE:

Did you make... love. Get children. I hear it actually happens to your kind.

SOCIAL WORKER:

So what does truth matter?

CASSANDRA:

I promised him I would... fuck, a silent fuck, but I broke my promise.

COP:

So what does truth matter?

MUSE:

Was Apollo angry with you then?

CASSANDRA:

For what I did he put a curse on and in me that no one would believe my words.

MUSES:

Oh, we believe you, everything you say.

JUDGES:

So what does truth matter?

MUSES:

(*laughing*) Oh we believe you, everything you say.

An audio mirage of voices will come on after each other.

SFX: (voiceover) I'll race you to the top of the hill... Dirty, dirty, dirty... I am sorry I am so old... You promised we'd always be together. Dirty, dirty, dirty. The thing is there is no place to land.

MUSES:

Oh we believe you everything you say. Oh we believe you, everything you say.

SFX: (voiceover) Tell us a story... you heard me... you heard us all, you heard us all the time, tell us a story... Sound of steps. Church bell ringing. Dirty, dirty, dirty. Hail Mary Full of Grace the Lord is with thee... steps...

CASSANDRA:

IT HURTS INSIDE MY HEAD! See there, see there above the school. Children like dreams, dead children, their flesh served up as meat for sacrifice which the Father ate and consumed with a hunger all his own. I have plotted revenge for this in my head and with my body, and oh MY lord, this female has fucked males, small deaths, at a time which have spermed a burst of a million swimming deaths closer to their own mortality.

MUSES:

Oh we believe you everything you say.

JUDGES:

So what does truth matter?

CASSANDRA:

You heard me cry out, and still you did not stop, You heard me cry out.

RAVEN:

AAAaaa! (*Raven screams*) Long festering feathers. GOD-DAMMIT!

MUSE:

Be silenced woman, do not speak of such ancient evil.

CASSANDRA:

The Gods who speak in me are me, are not always kind Gods.

MUSES:

Not if this is any indication.

CASSANDRA:

While you remain in your own self dark others plan to see.

MUSES:

What others?

CASSANDRA:

The power of those that see within and before and beyond.

MUSES:

Maybe, but I do not see how it could happen.

They exit slowly. She screams after them.

CASSANDRA:

You do not see me. You do not understand ME, you do not believe ME, because you do not believe anything, you are incapable of belief. (*Looks toward the light.*) And you Apollo, that great white bird, all enlightening God of Gods. Look... come close, look. This dress, why do I wear this dress? Picked out so carefully by you. All pressed proper against me so you can see me with you wide open blind eyes. Why do I wear this invisible wreath that pricks, pricks at my head still bloodying my mind with each thought. Take a look, take a look at all your pretty priestesses.

The Sisters appear in human form at the top of the stairs, they slowly descend.

SISTERS:

They watched me in my dresses the proper and the not so proper.

CASSANDRA:

And saw how I was laughed at by my friends and enemies.

SISTERS:

And how they hated me.

SISTER 1:

Me. Me. My love.

SISTER 2:

Me. Me. My life.

SISTERS:

Me. Me. My sex.

CASSANDRA:

Me. Me. My songs and words. And how he enjoyed it all. They said I was mad.

SISTERS:

Stark raving.

CASSANDRA:

Or a witch.

SISTERS:

Double, bubble, boil and bubble?

CASSANDRA:

Or a fortune teller.

SISTERS:

You shall marry a rich man, have a girl and boy and live a long life?

CASSANDRA:

And now my Apollo has finished with me.

Cassandra walks over to Raven, watching him.

RAVEN:

God-damn stubborn feathers... pluck... pluck... pluck. Awoo... awoo, shit.

CASSANDRA:

Here let me do that.

RAVEN:

Holy shit Cassandra. I... I... I didn't mea...

WISEGUY:

Nothing is gone for good, nothing (*smiles*).

CASSANDRA:

Let me guess, you didn't mean to. Believe this, I see you, bird boy. It doesn't matter how high you fly, I'll always be higher and out of reach.

RAVEN:

I don't want to fly. I want to land, on land, I want to land on land.

CASSANDRA:

Then see. Then look. Land on yourself and listen for the songs.

RAVEN:

I have no song.

CASSANDRA:

Let it come from you, all ancient and new. It's there rooted in you. You have a song. Sing it, so others might hear and know they are not alone, that we are all there in voices ancient and new, too many to be silenced.

RAVEN:

Sing it, so others might know they are not alone. Sing it.

Hecuba catches Cassandra's eye, she walks toward her. Hecuba appears on a higher level task at hand. She is taking and placing numerous dolls from her cart around her. Carefully with detail. Cassandra stops at Wiseguy's voice, approaches him as he talks to the Earth.

WISEGUY:

Exiled, we survived in our homeland. The smoke surrounding hides the waste made by ignorant, throwing spears, driving spears propelled by our own colourful brothers. We are here, we are not gone for good.

Cassandra begins to talk.

CASSANDRA:

I'm sor... You, SHHH now. I know you will be dancing and singing above me, feet touching the skies, your voice touching our hearts. I am lucky to be between two such women, two such worlds.

Hecuba looks down at them.

HECUBA:

Who the hell are you talking to?

WISEGUY:

Okay, three such woman. (*he laughs*)

Lights fade on Wiseguy. Hecuba sits dressing one of her dolls. Cassandra approaches her, Hecuba chooses to ignore her but talks to her through doll.

HECUBA:

There is no chance but life. Remember that. Now I know I stumble and fall on each tile of these streets, but at least I am upright some of the time. At least I AM still here fumbling with gravity. (*Cassandra goes to turn away. Hecuba talks intently to doll.*) There is hope, isn't there? Isn't there? If you love there is hope. Isn't there? Never, never will I let you go. I see your eyes in others and know that you are here in numbers that need to be mothered. (*She looks straight at Cassandra.*) Since your fears have made you defer to the stars, let a slave set you free from what you now still fear. Be bright, have no fear. I will manage. A siren I have always been, and a siren I will always be. (*She turns her attention to the doll and the chores of Hecuba's domesticity.*) That's it. That's it. Another child in the house. A house is not a home without children. Ask Mother Earth, we mothers do have our problems. Sit still now, aren't you the restless one? And just look at your hair. How many times have I told you? Brush your hair a...

CASSANDRA:
... hundred strokes before each night's sleep.

HECUBA:
... a hundred strokes before each night's sleep.

Cassandra kisses her on the cheek and leaves to carry on, up stairs. Hecuba carries on talking to her child.

HECUBA:
Now we'll name you Cassandra. That's it. That's it.

Hecuba dotes on her children. Cassandra reaches the top of the stairs. She turns and watches all three in their tasks.

Song:(Begins)

CASSANDRA:
As long as there have been stars. As long as I could hear them. As long as I have breathed I have known. The sky will be falling to take me back up.

Blueness gets brighter, stars appear.

Movement into dance either traditional and/ or a mixture of Trojan warrior movements similar to prologue but less fierce and more beautiful, flowing.

WISEGUY:
Look upon me, you who reflect upon me, and you hearers, hear me.

HECUBA:
Do not banish me from your sight.

RAVEN:

In my weakness, do not forsake me, and do not be afraid of my power.

SISTERS:

I am the members of the Great Mother.

CASSANDRA

I am she who exists in all fears and strength in the trembling.

HECUBA:

I am the solace of my labour pains.

WISEGUY:

We are the knowledge and ignorance. We are shame and boldness. We are shameless and we are ashamed. We are strength and we are fear. We are war and we are peace. Give heed to yourselves. We are all the disgraced and the great one.

Final drum beat, music stops, movements stop.

RAVEN

How you doing, sky?

SISTERS:

Fine, thank you.

RAVEN:

How are you Mother today?

Earth Woman points to him.

RAVEN:

Me? Just fine, thanks for asking.

WISEGUY:

Grandmother Moon. Kiss us, please.

END OF PLAY.

Photos taken at Margo Kane's workshop performance of
Confessions of an Indian Cowboy on June 24, 2001 in
Penticton, BC

photo credit: Greg Young-Ing

CONFESSIONS OF AN INDIAN COWBOY

by

Margo Kane

NOTES

The evolution of this script is still on going. This version will undergo more drafts. It is the nature of Margo's works to begin in an experimental state first which usually falls under the heading of Performance Art, although she never calls it that. The form is dependent on the content and the process of getting to the final work which will take shape as she writes and then performs, then writes and performs again. Her work is rooted in Oral Storytelling traditions and therefore improvisation is at the heart of her work. The story remains the same but the way it is told varies slightly with every telling. Margo spent many years in various community functions as a speaker, with the National Native Role Model Program. She likes to use the audience response as part of the show as a stand-up comedian might.

This performance moves back and forth between Ruby's consciousness and her memories of her family. The style of this piece was developed from Margo's way of script development that begins in the body as improvisation, with and without voice, with and without text. The extended movement is often non-literal and subsequently the movement for Ruby is her text; just as the other characters use a hybrid of Aboriginal storytelling and *Commedia 'del Arte clown* characters to share their perspectives.

NOTES ON MUSIC

With the exception of a few tunes listed, the Music was composed by Barrie Nighswander (guitarist), Doug Thordarson (fiddler) and Joseph "Pepe" Danza (percussionist).

MUSIC CREDITS

Angel from Montgomery
Songwriter: Prine, Performers: John Prine and Bonnie Raitt, Published by Sour Grapes Music and Walden Music Inc. (WB Music)

Halfbreed
Songwriter: Mary Dean and Al Capps, Performer: Cher, Published by Blue Monday Music

Mama's Don't let your Babies Grow up to Be Cowboys
Songwriter: Patsy Anne Bruce, Performer: Willie Nelson, Published by Sony ATV Tree Music Publishing, Sony ATV Tree Music Publishing Canada

CAST OF CHARACTERS
(All characters are played by one actor)

RUBY:	daughter of Rodeo Princess and Cowboy Dad
KOKUM:	Ruby's grandmother
OLD MAN:	Kokum's husband
INDIAN COWBOY	Uncle
COWBOY DAD:	non-Aboriginal construction boomer
RODEO PRINCESS:	Ruby's Mother

ACT I.

The Musicians sit Upstage Left. A fiddler, guitarist and a percussionist are dressed as a Métis voyageur, a Cowboy and an Indian.

The Setting:

A large fence stands Upstage Right draped with costumes and props: blankets, shawls, cowboy boots and a Western saddle is strapped to it as well. Downstage Left is a stump beside a rock campfire with coffee pot and tin camping cup and a paperback novel from Louis L'Amour's collection.

The character Kokum (Grandmother) and Old Man (one and the same character) are entering through the audience, visiting and chatting with audience, sitting with them during the pre-show live music. The live music finishes and the play and new music begins.

MUSIC: Round Dance Song.

KOKUM/OLD MAN
I'M WALKIN' ROUND DANCE

Begins in audience offstage and enters chanting to music. Begins text and punctuates it with chanting throughout.

Costume – Hudson's Bay coat, gum boots, Kokum's skirt underneath.

OLD MAN:

(sings and chants)

 I'm walkin'
 walkin' down the long Red Road
 paddlin' up clear blue rivers
 haulin' my canoe over the portage through the bush.
 my pony draggin' the travois behind.

 I've been walkin' this land for an eternity.
 I am as old as the hills
 as old as the dust on my boots.
 Old as the mud I'm sinkin' into,
 sinkin' down into the mud of the earth.

 as old as the cedars
 the cedars cut down in that forest you call Stanley Park
 we call it woejdojfkjfoflk;lskpfapoelfmsm!
 why you have to rename everything?

 all creation and all its creatures know me
 I run with the buffalo
 I dance with the deer
 I play with the antelope
 I burrow with the groundhog.
 Twitter and tweet with the black bird.

 Reprise:
 I'm walkin' down the long red road
 paddlin' clear blue rivers
 I'm walkin'

KOKUM:

(sings and chants)

 Okay ol' man you've had your say. Enough already.

 Walking the Red Road.
 Walking and singing on my way.
 I walk feet firmly on the good earth.
 I'm walkin' in two worlds. That's a cliche if I ever heard one.

My memory is as long and as old as the earth under my feet.
We been walking this earth long before the visitors came.
We never forgot how we helped them through the long hard winters.
We never forgot our families,
how they left them for their homes back in the old world.
Our memory is long and as old as the earth under our feet.

Following the path worn by the moccasins of my ancestors.
The path that my ancestors walked.
Walking the Red Road.
Walking and singing on my way.

MUSIC OUT

RUBY
WHICH PATH?

MUSIC: Tangled Underbrush

Soundscape fades in slowly.

Ruby removes Kokum's skirt and shawl, scarf slides around neck. Places them reverently over fence, memories of her family and their stories rise to the surface of her mind. She crosses to campfirefire, crosses to water pail, drinks from the dipper, then lets the rest of water dribble into the pail. Looks around.

RUBY:

Is anybody there? Hello.*(movement throughout)* This way and that way. Every which way. I walk. My feet. Footprints... deep. Into the earth. I pray for a path to emerge. Muddy footprints. My thoughts are tangled underbrush, winding around each other, impossible to see a way out of this. Show me a way that doesn't trail off into more bramble bushes. Trails that fork. Which way? I run until I can go no farther. I retrace my steps.

MUSIC: Tangled Underbrush

Soundscape changes to small pony score throughout next running sequence.

I run. (*she runs*) I run. (*she runs in another direction*) I run. (*She runs in another direction, then begins to run around the whole stage, changing direction as if she is a horse caught in a corral.*)

RUBY
SMALL PONY

RUBY:

(*neighing several times*) I am a small pony. A wild mustang, I roam in a herd of ponies of many colours. Many sizes and shapes. We run together. (*neighing as a horse and running and leaping throughout the space*) We gallop for hours, for miles and miles. Leaping over treefalls, crumbling stonewalls and small ditches full of rain water. We head into the hills. The dust billowing behind us, manes and tails flying. Look Ma no hands! (*rides with both hands over her head round and round centre stage*)

MUSIC: finishes and changes to forest sounds.

We graze in meadows, moving where the fresh grass is following familiar trails to our hidden drinking pools. The willows, the smell of moist earth, the tinkling of water rippling over the rocks. (*has moved to waterpail and drinks from dipper*) Tasting the clear, cool water. The air moving. Breathing. The sun filtering through the leaves. The tree roots clearing the ground, the hollows beneath the trees. Where the forest people, the little people, live.

RUBY
ON THE EDGE

MUSIC: galloping changes to edgy soundscape.

RUBY:

And we're off across the fields, along dusty roads, finding our way through the woods on the edge of town. Tangled underbrush. On the edge of town. On the edge, the edge, the edge, the edge, on the edge. I'm, I'm on the edge!

MUSIC OUT

The Canyon. Standing on the edge, the shadow of myself leaves my body to leap over the edge. My breath catches in my throat. Dark clouds gathering. Icy wind blowing, overwhelming silence replacing the birds as they fly in retreat. This place, filled with things unsaid; criticism, voices of judgment creep out of the brooding silence. Run for cover. Can't go home. Home? This isn't home anymore.

In the canyon below the bullets ricochet back and forth. I manage to keep my cover till dusk falls, abandon the battle to fight another day. It's the same old story! Like the Cowboys and the Indians. The old us and them. What are we fighting for?

INDIAN COWBOY
THOSE WERE THE DAYS

MUSIC: Open Skies, along with nature sounds.

Costume – Indian Cowboy dresses into boots, chaps, hat with braids while the telephone rings insistently.

INDIAN COWBOY:
Somebody get that damn phone! What a day, nice and peaceful, quiet. Can stand on the bluff and look to Herman's chunka land out there, just a grove of balsam and spruce trees around the house. Ol' Massey Fergusen, shell of a Galaxie 500 – could carry alotta Indians in its day, an ol' frigidaire, door ajar. Yeh, it was real purdy. Yeh, you can smell the fresh hayin' meadows and sometimes the wind blowin' the scent of the lake, down at the bottom of the gulch. The paddocks, corrals, and the barns over ta Ol Man Marlowe's. The whinnying of his rangy herd a mustangs, with a few horses from the track thrown in for good

measure. Nothing like standing at sunset and watchin' the dusk settle in.

Different country when I worked the ranches, over to Alberta...

Crosses stage to campfire

MUSIC: Faded Love

... moving from job to job until I gotta hankerin' for settlin' down. There the land stretches for miles and miles. In the fall, you'd be drivin' back from Fort MacLeod at dusk and you'd hit a rise in those rollin' hills. The dust rising off the hayfields and the machinery lights for miles around as everyone brought in their harvest. The dust changing colour with the sunfall and those big lights reflectin' on the fields. They'd go all night, as long as it would take.

MUSIC: Red River Valley

OLD MAN
PUSHED OUT

Costume – Old Man in coat. Boots and chaps stay on. Add skirt.

OLD MAN:
There was good buffalo huntin' before they came along. Our people been waitin' for some kind of restitution from the government for a long time now. For all the land they took and the buffalo they killed and the way of living they destroyed by their expansion and their railroad and their greediness and their thievery. Their thievery of land and property that didn't really belong to them. They pushed us out.

MUSIC OUT

Oh you know, a lotta people used to go down to visit their relatives, take their Red River carts down, chase buffalo, stateside, especially when ours were all gone. And some were given pieces of land so they would settle down and become farmers, but farmin's not for everybody. And some bought into those treaties and were virtual prisoners on some pitiful piece a land. Others just made a quick getaway and eluded the law forever. They found relatives stateside or just stayed outta reach for as long as they could, outta reach of the Indian agents and government officials.

Mostly they just moved west to continue their way of life. Travel where the game was. It was west and more west. The country was being developed and finally many people ended up livin' in the road allowances. The government had already parcelled up the land and they couldn't be squattin' on anybody's land, now could they, without some kinda trouble. So they squatted in the road allowance, heh? They were allowed to go into town sometimes, but they were treated with lots of suspicion. They'd come into town, only on certain days of the week, when they were allowed to and they'd return to their carts in the road allowances at night. Some managed to pick up odd jobs. They had to take what scraps they could get, what odd jobs were available to them. They laboured alongside other poor sods that been flooding into the country. Yah, it wasn't easy.

KOKUM
MY HUSBAND

Costume – Old Man removes coat revealing Kokum who takes scarf from around neck and covers her head, tying it under her chin.

Kokum moves cross stage to sit on stump at campfire. She drinks from tin cup and stares off for awhile before speaking.

KOKUM:

My husband was a good man... a good man, not like all those other yahoos, you know the ones I mean. Yah, he worked hard. Kept them traplines in good workin' order. Sometimes we didn't know when he was gonna come home. He always brought us somethin'; a nice fat hare, couple a muskrats, some-

287

times a white-faced heifer. Jus' jokin'.

Times got kinda tough, ya know. We kept movin'. We liked to move anyways. They were movin' that darn railway, iron horse ya know. We had some good times. Pretty good times. We'd load up the carts and go down stateside, camping with our relatives from all over, the last buffalo runs. Oh, sure good times then. He was a great buffalo hunter.

My old man, his family was movin' eh? Movin' out west. He picked up odd jobs when he could. He was a good worker. Good with his hands. Sure was good with his hands. Ranchin' stuff, you know. Ropin' and brandin' and such. Good man. (*she puts cup down and stands*)

KOKUM
BUFFALO BILL JOKE

KOKUM:

Did you hear the one about the two cowboys riding across the prairies? One was an ol' timer, Buffalo Bill, kinda old and crooked, you know, one too many round ups (*wink*). And the other one, his new partner, just a young buck, ya know. A rookie. Fresh outta gun slingin' school. Got hisself a fancy twin gun and holster set and he's itchin' to use 'em. He's got the full get up, eh. The boots and spurs, and he got them chaps, you know. Those big angora chaps. Real fancy, eh. And the ol' timer, he mounts his pony and beckons to his new partner. "Git!" And they header outta town. Out into the prairies beyond. And Bill settles into his saddle for a long, easy ride, hees hat low on hees head hopin' for a little shuteye. And this young buck he's rarin' to git goin', eh. He's just a given 'er with them guns. He's lookin' for a jackrabbit, or an old lame coyote to chase across the prairie, eh? Lookin' and lookin'. Practisin' his scouting skills.

A while later, the dude sees somethin' behind 'em. It's a small figure on the horizon! And he squints into the light. And whadda ya know, it's an Indian! BIG feather! A sweat breaks out on his upper lip. His free hand goes to one a' them guns. His horse starts dancin' underneath him. Whoa there, Nellie! And Ol Bill wakes with a start. "What's all the commotion?" And the young buck waves his gun in the Indian's direction. (*stammering*) "Indian! BIG..." (*gesturing feather*) Ol' Bill, "How big is he?" "He's about this big!" (*shows 1 inch size with his thumb and finger*) "Well, he's a long ways off. Just keep your eye on him."

So for the next while, that young feller is a twistin' and a turnin' in his saddle, and shore 'nough, hee's followin' 'em! He says to Ol' Bill in a hoarse whisper, "Lemme ride over to them hills and swing around and come up behind him. I can take him out." But Ol' Bill says, "How big is he now?" "About this high." (*still uses one hand to show a height of 3 inches*) "Ahh, just hold your horses, don't seem to me he'd be any trouble." And he rides on. Boy, that young feller is about to pee hisself cause that Indian is still shadowin' 'em, just keepin' a safe distance. Finally he can't handle the suspense anymore and he squeaks in Bill's ear, "I gotta clean shot. Lemme at 'im!" Ol' Bill relents, "Aw, g'wan! Shoot 'im!" The kid pulls out both his pistols, aims and freezes. "What's a matter?" "I can't." "Whaddyah mean ya can't?" "I can't, I know'd him since he was this high." (*demonstrating an inch high with his thumb and finger*)

MUSIC: Happy Mud

RUBY

Costume – Changes out of wardrobe and takes Kokum's shawl and dances like a child to Music.

RUBY:

I'm coming! I'm coming! When we were kids, we spent a lot of time with Kokum, driving her to town for groceries, canning vegetables and fruit, playing bingo! We would go with her berry picking down by the river, in the mudflats. And we'd bury our feet in the mud. Squishing them back and forth, seeing how deep we could get. Mud! In a pool of mud, squishing between our toes, above our ankles, our calves. Oh, I'm gonna fall!

KOKUM:

You kids! Get outta that river, or I'll tan your hides!

MUSIC: Happy Mud Out

RUBY
MY MOTHER

RUBY:

We loved to dress up in her clothes, her jewellry, her scarves and her shawls and parade up and down like we were in a fashion show. (*she parades around like a model*) Kokum said I looked a lot like my mom. She put on her own fashion shows. She could sing and dance and she won all the talent contests. I have a picture of her in her Indian costume in her beads and feathers and her dress with long fringes. She was the Second Runner Up for the Indian Powwow Princess Pageant at home. After she started hanging around with them cowboys she became the All Nations Galaxy Indian Rodeo Princess of 1965.

MUSIC: Witchy Woman.

RODEO PRINCESS/MOM
WINNING MY CROWN

Costume – Changes into white cowboy boots, fancy blue shawl, and white cowboy hat throughout following monologue.

RODEO PRINCESS/MOM:

When I won my crown, I was invited all over the countryside to every Indian Rodeo that was happening. I won a big silver belt buckle. And a whole new outfit. With new boots! I got to ride in parades, and kiss babies and shake hands with all kinds of people. And I got to smile a lot and make pretty speeches. (*steps onto stump to speak*) Well I'm coming to end of my year as Miss All Nations Galaxy Indian Rodeo Princess of 1965. Thank you, thank you, thank you, it's been an incredible year. (*she is getting very dramatic*) And as I travel I see how large our communities have grown and how we can take over this fair land that was always ours anyways. Oops. (*music stops abruptly then begins again*) Thank you. Thank you. (*Cameras flash as she poses and throws kisses to audience. Music finishes with a flourish*)

KOKUM:

(*says to band*) It was enough that she was gallavantin' all over the countryside. But when she finished her whirlwind tour, she was galavantin' off every Friday and Saturday night with her girl friends. All gussied up, blue eye shadow. You can't go out of this house looking like that! No good comes of the girls down at the Royal Hotel!

RUBY:

And is that where you first met my Dad?

MUSIC: Golden Slippers

PRINCESS:

(*Sashaying and dancing about with shawl. Exchanges her hat for Cowboy Dad's hat on fence.*) Oh, that was a long time ago. When I first laid eyes on him, he had a rucksack over his shoulder, a big stetson-like hat, and a smile and a tip of his hat to every lady that passed. He was a perfect gentleman!

COWBOY DAD
ROYAL HOTEL

Cowboy Dad puts on Duster coat and removes a pouch of tobacco from the pocket. He rolls a cigarette which he hangs from his lower lip while he continues his monologue.

COWBOY DAD:

I was a hard worker, just like any one of the boys. You know, you do a good days work, ya git paid, have a little fun. Come in from a big job out in the boonies. Us boys would roll in with big fat cheques after bein' outta town for sometime. You gotta cash 'em somewhere. In them days the banks weren't open Saturdays. But we'd roll into town and head for the Royal Hotel. They were top-notch. They'd cash our payroll cheques for all us boys! An' they would be holdin' a lot of money for us. I'll tell ya, that Royal Hotel was one of the few hotels round there that never got robbed, because they knew there'd be trouble from us boys. We'd give 'em what fer! (*puts up dukes and shadow-boxes*) They liked our business.

I sees her enter the room with her girlfriends. Heads are turnin' every which way to take a gander. Some of the boys aren't afraid to sashay on up to them, strike-up a conversation that could lead to a turn or two around the dance floor. But I've got two left feet so I just keep an eye on her through the night. She's a pretty little filly, tossing her mane and kickin' up her heels. Her dance card is mighty full, I'd say. And then, Geez! She walks right up to me and asks me to dance.

Music gets faster. They dance, two stepping, square dancing, twirling.

MUSIC OUT as he throws his hat in air with a coyote yell.

KOKUM
CURSIN' COWBOYS

Round Dance

Costume change from cowboy Dad to Kokum, with scarf, boots off and shawl, while beginning chant with band.

MUSIC: Round Dance beginning with drum. Then layering in other instruments over costume change.

KOKUM:

You stay away from that cowboy! You gotta watch them cowboys! He's gonna let you down. He's gonna leave like they all do. Once they got what want, they go back to where they came from and marry their own people.

Don't come into this house with those dirty boots! Just, look at that dirt. Damn cowboys trackin' mud into my kitchen. Take your hat off in the house.

Them cowboys! They ride into our territory, stakin' claims to anything that ain't tied down, but of course they only want the choice land. Christopher Columbus! Who do they think they are anyways? I don't cotton much to them cowboys, drinkin' and shootin', and spittin' everywhere.

MUSIC OUT

RUBY:

I guess that was one battle Kokum lost, cause here I am. I remember asking Kokum. Where do family trees grow? Do we have one?

KOKUM
INTERMARRIAGE I

KOKUM:

No, we don't have a family tree. We got family bushes, bramble bushes, tangled overgrown bramble bushes. I'm warning you it ain't a pretty story. There was a rumour in our family my great aunt was cohortin', no, consortin', no it was fraternizin' with the Chinese, and out came Auntie Bea. Little woman with almond shaped eyes. And then there was Uncle Billy. Now there was a Cree dandy. I got an old picture from the forties. Suit and tie, his shoes all buffed. He came from a surveyor of the Hudson's Bay Company. And a Cree woman: Swampy Cree, Saulteaux and French. Enough to make his head curl! Then there was Jack who married my first daughter. And his family were mostly a mixture of dirt poor Irish, Scottish, and English. They came looking for a new beginning as the country was opening up. Not many jobs in them days except making roads and highways, digging ditches and sewers for towns. Workin', playin' and marrying one another! They were all family.

RUBY
HALFBREED

RUBY:

Oh, great! I am a mutt! I was born an Indian but sometimes I wanted to be the Cowboy. I wanted to be the hero! And now it's not enough that I'm a mongrel but my father is a cowboy and my mother an Indian. What does that makes me? A Halfbreed!! Where do I belong?

Do you know what it feels like to have someone say:

Cowboy: You're an Indian? You don't look like an Indian.
Indian: Why you dressed like that? Who you trying to be?

Cowboy: Can't you tell us something about your culture and traditions that we haven't already read about?
Indian: You're not an Indian – you didn't grow up on the reserve.

Cowboy: Do you have any great chiefs or medicine people in your family tree?
Indian: You call yourself an Indian? You don't even like salmon.

Cowboy: You use a computer, that's not traditional.
Indian: You think like a white man.

Cowboy: I'm tired of all you Indians living on welfare at our expense.
Indian: You've never suffered. You've always lived off reserve.

Cowboy: Get off your butts and work for a living like every-one else in this country.

OLD MAN
FIGHTING WORDS

OLD MAN:

(*grabs coat and starts shadowboxing*) Them's fightin' words! Put up your dukes! Don't you come in here and tell me how to run things. You just watch your p's and q's or we're gonna run you out on a rail. We don't like your kind around here. You go back to where you came from. Git in them stinkin' boats and sail back to the old world. Gave them a piece of my mind. There was good buffalo huntin' till they came along!

RUBY
SINKING INTO MUD

RUBY:

Where's the sun? The light has gone from the world, leaving grey shadows. Days upon days of shadows. Hovering around me. Pooling around my feet, a dark puddle growing. Rising, sinking. The black muck oozing through my toes at the bottom. Mired in muck. My feet sinking through the muck at the bottom. Sinking to my calf, sinking to my knees. This blackness growing all around me. I don't want to go on. I don't want to go on like this. Let me sink. The earth will swallow me up in the black muck. (*begins to chant*)

MUSIC: chant with drum.

INDIAN COWBOY
PONY

INDIAN COWBOY:

Those ponies sure are pretty. You know a good pony is worth his weight in gold; found me one wild from the Cypress Hills. Never skittish, brave hearted, a damn good cow pony. There was not a heifer he couldn't pull out of the mud after a rain storm. I could always count on him. When you got a good pony you're set for life.

MUSIC: soundscape of sneak-up to horse capture.

Indian Cowboy starts to stalk a herd with his buddies and soon he's waving a blanket over his head, chasing the horses and hollering after them to keep them running into the canyon, and the ponies race down and are caught in the canyon.

Music fading.

One pony left in the canyon below. I move out from the shadow of the boulder. The pony runs back and forth. I place my feet firmly on the packed earth. I avoid eye contact. He runs towards me, teeth barred and stops only a few feet from me. I stand still. I have watched my Elders. Their breath in the horses nostrils. Their reassuring voices. It won't be long till I have gentled my pony. On his back, guiding him with only one small rope and my knees. Learning each other's language.

MUSIC: Open Skies

Riding round and round that rock canyon before moving out onto the prairie. Standing and looking up to the sky. Watching the sunset together. That one horse, only me on his back.

MUSIC: Open Skies crescendos to finish Act 1.

END OF ACT I.

ACT II

MUSIC: Cheatin' Heart.

OLD MAN
RADIO SHOW

Costume – skirt and Hudson's Bay coat and rubbers

Ol' Man enters looking lost.

OLD MAN:

How did I get here? Yeh, been here, been here before. So many things I can't remember anymore. Ah, it don't matter though, I tell better stories than what really happened anyway. Oh yeh. How do ya like my new boots? (*limping towards stump*) Kinda stiff. Ol' buffalo huntin' injury. Crow River. That's another story. (*sits at DJ booth and places head phones on his head*)

Well hello, all you listeners out there! This is your favourite disc jockey Melvin Snowshoe, comin' live from our station, deep in the muskeg of the Northern Territories. How are you today? I just have a few things I need to get off my chest today and I will be takin' your phone calls later on in the program. You were just listening to Hank Williams, one of our favourite cowboys, singin' about Your Cheatin' Heart. On that note, Billy Brady, stop your tomcattin' around! We all know what's goin' on, don't we?

Now for the next order of business. Sadie Descheneaux has notified us that she's gathered all her medicines now, so you can drop on by and have a cup a tea with her. She likes to hear the news ya know and she's always got some good Indian bannock to treat you with. Just like the ol' days. People used to stop by all the time. Now they only telephone when they want something!

You know I got me a few new tunes for ya today. This one reminds me of the days when our people paddled for the fur companies. That's hard work, paddlin' up river with a huge canoe full of supplies and trade goods. Their packs full of pemmican, you know, buffalo tallow, and berries and what have you. After all that time out on the rivers and in the back countries, they would come in together to celebrate. It was a time when all people could get together; the French, the Indians, the Scottish and Irish. They'd dance all night. They'd dance till they wore out their moccasins.

You know a lot of the fiddlers back in them days, they didn't have a lot of trainin', those Indian fiddlers. They learned from the French and the Scottish and Irish folks who they worked side by side with. So they weren't formally trained but, they say they tuned their fiddles to the cry of the loon and the bellow of the rutting moose. Mmm. Well here's a thought for you. If anyone can imitate the bellow of a ruttin' moose, I want you to call in. Maybe it will attract some more moose into our country and we won't have to worry about food for the rest of the winter!

Who's out there? ... Oh! oh sure. (*talking to his wife*) Pardon me folks but we've got a visitor who dropped by to make a little service announcement.

MUSIC: Hokee Indian sounds.

KOKUM
HOW TO BE AN INDIAN

KOKUM:
Well, I think there oughtta be a class on, 'How to be an Indian.' I wonder if I should put it together down at the Community Centre. Cause you know, there's a lot of misconceptions about being an Indian. And the first misconception we're not really

Indians! You know all about Christopher Columbus? He thought he'd discovered the Indies so he called us Indians. So that's the first thing we'd be talking about in this class.

Now the second thing, stems from the first, and that is there are many different kinds of Indians with as many different languages. (*names a few languages*) And there are them that use a mix of Indian, French and English and have created their own language. And let's not forget Indian sign language. (*hand signing*) MOOSE! (*signs again*) BULLSHIT! Or This! (*gesturing with lips*) You're pointing at that fellow over there? Doesn't mean your trying to kiss him, no. (*points in direction with head motion to one side*) How about you and me take a walk... for a coke!

Yep, there are plenty more lessons where they came from but I don't want to give it all away all at once. One last note: this class is not just for Indians; it's for Cowboys too!

MUSIC: Hokee reprise.

OLD MAN
CONTINUED RADIO SHOW

OLD MAN:
That woman is never at a loss for words. Now here's a song I'm sure you'll like!

MUSIC: Big John McNeil.

Oh, that's my kinda fiddlin'! Now everyone remember the weddin' dance this Saturday night down at the community hall. Congratulations Pearl and Gunther Many Beavers. I hope you got them fiddlers tunin' up them fiddles cause we're gonna be down there in our jiggin' boots and our moccasins and our fancy clothes to celebrate your weddin'. Oh yeh, that's the kinda music I like. (*Old Man dances a jig*)

Costume – removes coat and skirt.

MUSIC: Kokum's Lament

Kokum with Rodeo Princess Blue Shawl to four directions before kneeling to grave side. Music changes when finished four directions.

RUBY
WHEN MOMMA DIED

RUBY:

When Momma died, there were a lot of people coming and going. I would hide in her room and lay on her bed and try to imagine her laying there. I couldn't believe she left us so soon. I saw her moving around the room, sitting at her dressing table, opening her closet to choose a special outfit. When Momma died, I remember my sisters going through the house, pulling the doilies and the knick-knacks off the tables, chattering and arguing, and tugging at this and that. I crawled into her closet to get away from their voices. Like crows squabbling!

MUSIC: Bluesy beats

(*crawls out under fence and looks into coffin*) Can you hear me? Are you up there, somewhere, or over here, over there. (*cross stage*) I want to look at death. Or not. The death of someone you love, it hovers...

MUSIC OUT

... or is it following me... as I walk. (*walks away, faster and faster and turns into pony and runs*)

MUSIC: Running Pony

RUBY/GIRL
I WANTED TO BE A COWBOY

RUBY/GIRL:

Easy Boy! Easy! (*end of run – music slows then stops*) When I was a boy, well a tomboy, I wanted to be a cowboy. Not a cowgirl. I wanted to have a hat, a twin gun holster set, chaps, and boots with spurs, cha-ching, cha-ching, cha-ching! (*strolls around like a cowboy while musicians make spur cha-ching*) I knew how to handle them ornery varmints. I would just give'em a long piercing look (*Looks at musicians who have their guns pointed at her. They slowly drop their guns.*) and leave the room without a word. Cha-ching, cha-ching, cha-ching. (*Musicians begin to guffaw and snicker at her. She stomps away*) I ain't a girl! I'm a cowboy. So there! My father isn't a ditch digger, he's a cowboy! He's outta on the range, roundin' up little doggies gone astray!

Snickering. Ends with Stomping out.

COWBOY DAD
CONSTRUCTION BOOMER

COWBOY DAD:

(*puts on Duster coat*) Guys like me had to move where the work was. We were outta town sometimes six weeks at a time. Digging ditches for sewer pipes, laying foundations for new towns, bridges, building highways. A construction boomer. Yeh, I liked getting outta town. Hoppin' on the first train headin' into the mountains, pickin' up jobs in places I'd never seen before. Enjoyed the freedom, the adventure, headin' into new territories. I liked the forests and mountains, but it was the deserts that really grabbed me. I always had a real hankerin' to header over stateside to take a gander at their deserts. Maybe that's one of the reasons that I love the frontier. A place where no one has been before, or touched with their machinery. (*chuckling*) And I loved those ol' Frontier stories, all kinds of renegades and outlaws and full of action. Like Louis L'Amour. (*picks up book at campfire and rests foot on stump while reading*)

MUSIC: The Good, the Bad and the Ugly

My name is Ryan Tyler. (*reading from pocketbook*) and people say I killed twenty-seven men. The fact is, I killed just ten, every man jack of them in a stand-up fair fight. And that goes for Indians as well, though nobody counted Indians in those days.

Some people say I was all bad. That I killed without reason. That I was an outlaw. They say that no man has a right to kill another man. That's why I'm writing this all down so you can judge for yourself.

My feeling is my guns and some other guns made it easier for those who came later. The cattle roam fat and lazy now, people sleep well at night. The guns are hung up and I think they've got people like me to thank for it.

MUSIC OUT

(L'Amour, Louis. To Tame a Land. Fawcett Publications, Inc., Greenwich. 1955)

COWBOY DAD
Come on, little missy, I got the tickets. Let me give you a leg up.

Ruby tears Duster coat off as a child scrambling to climb into saddle strapped to fence.

RUBY
PONY RIDES

RUBY:
The first pony I ever rode was on the carousel. (*Carousel music*) The merry-go-round we called it. Going up and down and up and down and music playing all the while, and your daddy standing beside you. And up and down, the wind

blowing through your hair, in your face, as the merry-go-round goes up and down, up and down.

There was no music on the next horse that I rode. At the Safeways or the IGA. For a dime, (*machine horse music*) a cowboy could do an easy canter or a hell-bent gallop if you pulled the reins hard enough. Sitting on a real leather saddle with leather stirrups on a little motorized horse, surveying the lands stretched out, out into the parking lot.

The next horse was real! Live ponies at the fairgrounds! (*music of ponies*) They go round and round, in a circle, hooked to a big wheel-thing. Dad's or mom's walking beside the kids, plodding along. I loved the smell of the pony and the squeak of the leather saddle. I never wanted to get off. I wanted to plod on and on, forever. (*falls asleep in saddle*)

Climbing off pony. Changes

RUBY:
When is Daddy coming home?

KOKUM:
I don't have the foggiest notion.

RUBY:
He's been gone a long time now.

KOKUM:
Here. Take this to the trash. (*to herself*) Just like all those other cowboys wandering off in search of another frontier – a new woman, another family. It is so easy for men to walk away from their responsibilities.

Costume – Changes out of chaps, hat. Adds shawl and remember-ing daughter she holds shawl as if it is a baby. She rocks it and chants to the baby. Chant turns into melody

MUSIC: Mama Don't Let Your Babies Grow Up To Be Cowboys

RUBY
FALLEN ANGEL

End of song, Ruby runs with the shawl.

RUBY:

Sometimes I would fly across the grass and I would stumble and fall and collapse on the grass and just lay there. I lay dead... (*sound of flutes and rattles*) my eyes wide open starring to the sky. I felt the earth beneath me. I heard the twittering of the birds, the buzz of the insects, the flutter of the dragon fly above me. The smell of the earth and the grass, heated by the sun. My eyes open. I lay very still. Some fallen angel.

MUSIC OUT

MUSIC: Cajun Summer

INDIAN COWBOY
OPEN SKIES

INDIAN COWBOY:

Reach, reach up. See the open sky. The clouds race with the winds. The smell of fresh rain as the winds shift, gathering the storm behind. The bawling of calves and their mothers. See the wind, see the wind pushing and shoving, and coaxing and urging the clouds. The smell of the rain coming in on the wind. Thunder Beings rolling across the foothills. Across the fields, you can smell it coming.

RUBY
WAITIN' OUT THE STORM

RUBY:

Hello, is anyone there? Gotta go. Gotta move on. Itching to go. Which way? Every which way. This way, that way, just don't know. Where will we go? Where will we end up? Why go? Is there no easy, simple way? Wait. There must be a right way. Think. Don't wait too long, gotta go!

My thoughts tumbling around like stones. Stones being washed away. Tumbling rocks along the creek, rushing between canyon walls. Tumbling over one another.

Fresh hail from the sky. Stinging, zinging, hammering on a tin roof, the pelting of a sudden hail. I can't see. I can't see! (MUSIC: Storm Fade Begins) Wait. Wait til the storm decreases. Wait if you can, stay right where you are, don't move, don't try and find the way, just stay put, stay wherever you are. Stay alive! Stay high and dry if you can.

MUSIC: Storm fades

RUBY
NO MORE BATTLE/HOLLOW IN THE GROUND

RUBY:

The battle is too fierce.
I feel I'm losing the battle.
Lost before I even begin.
It's impossible.
I'm unable to take a stand.

I want to run.
Flee to the hills, the bush
I want to run as far as I can
I don't want to fight any longer.
No more!
I want them to hear me.
I want them to lay down their weapons.

I feel frightened. Tired of this constant battle.
Constant arguments
Constant refusal by both camps to listen
Constant refusal to lay down weapons
I am despairing that the battle will never end.

I want to retreat.
Retreat into the bush.
To get as far away as I can from the sound of cannons, the

smell of battle, the rivers of blood.
I want to leave this place.

This battle is never-ending. It never quits. Why don't I just lay down in a little hollow in the ground and let the rain and the wind overtake me. No More. No more.

MUSIC: Angel From Montgomery sung with Band and Kokum/Rodeo Princess/Ruby

OLD MAN
WHEN DEATH COMES WALKING IN YOUR DOOR

Costume – Skirt, scarf, red boots and coat

He slowly moves across stage to sit on stump.

OLD MAN:

When death comes walking in your door. You pretend you don't see him. You don't acknowledge him, how he looks, or what he wears, or how he acts. Maybe, when death comes walking in your door, he's only a very faint presence, but maybe you feel him at some moment and you push him away. You think your minds playing tricks. And once your loved ones have left you, you begin to look for ways to be prepared for the next time around. And you try to spend more time with your loved ones. And you tell them how you feel about them and how wonderful they are. And talk of the things you used to do together. And you tell old stories again that you been telling back and forth to each other, over and over through the years. And you phone them every week, or every other day. And find time to talk about things, find ways to talk about difficult things and things that aren't easily explainable. When death comes walking, you're prepared. Yes you are. As prepared as any one can be, I suppose.

It was that way with the buffalo, one minute there were herds and more herds, movin' cross the lands. And the next you had to travel a far ways to find a herd and pretty soon there were no buffalo at all. The skulls were piled in huge mounds 30 feet high. And it happened so fast. We never knew what we had until it was gone, we never saw it coming.

KOKUM
WHO WILL REMEMBER?

KOKUM:

There's time for this. Time for that. A time for every season under heaven. What do you want? Indian wisdom?

I don't know nothin'. I keep my feet planted firmly on the good earth. I walk bare footed, through the grass, I let my toes trail in the fresh flowing creeks, I feel the mud from the river bank oozing up between my toes, And I feel my roots sink deep into this earth. Now-a-days, it's hard to look around and see the wild bush tamed by fields and fences, roads and powerlines. Once the tree roots are dug up, and piled with the burning brush, all that's left is the wood pile in the shed. Who will remember? Who will remember what was here now that it's gone?

RUBY
ALLEGIANCES

RUBY:

I remember being caught in the cross fire. I remember the stench of the dead. The blood stained river. People falling on every side of me. The forced marches, huddling together for warmth in thin blankets, dwindling food rations. I remember begging on the edge of town. Standing in a graveyard of losses; the loss of feelings, words, languages, peoples, of creatures that fly and swim and crawl and walk the earth, the lands, the territories.

I live with this confusion, this tension in a world that wants me to declare some allegiance to one side or the other. How can I when the blood of all my ancestors flows like tributaries of that great river. Flows into the river of my blood. Sings as clear rippling streams over smooth round stones, (*MUSIC: drumbeat*) smooth round stones bouncing along with currents as old as the

canyons along which they speed, currents that carve out path-
ways through soft sedentary rock, rock that is varied in its min-
eral content, as varied as the kinds of life it supports, the blood
is as varied as... the music (*MUSIC: add fiddle and guitar*)
which my father's father carried with him from his Irish Scot's
homelands, that mingled with the drum and chant from my
mother's people, the Cree and the Saulteaux. The dance which
was shared around cold winter nights, the camps alive with
their frolicking, camps alive with camaraderie despite their dif-
ferences. This is what I want to remember.

MUSIC: Round Dance Chant.

KOKUM
CULTURAL PURITY

KOKUM:

I don't understand all this commotion about cultural purity.
Everyone's on the bandwagon tryin' to prove their pure-blood-
ed this an' that! I don't know when the last time you checked
your woodpile but from earliest times our people have been
tradin' and travellin' with and marryin' into each other's families: the French, the English, the Spanish, the Blacks, the
Chinese, the Irish, the Scots, the Catholics, the Mormons, the
Pentacostals, the Anglicans, the Unitarians... NEED I SAY
MORE!

Round Dance out

MUSIC: Cajun Summer

INDIAN COWBOY
MOVIN' CAMP

INDIAN COWBOY:

Same old story. You're on the edge of a new frontier. Havin' to
move out into new territory; movin' camp. Not knowin' where
you might end up, or what challenges you'll have to face.
Whadda you take with you? Whadda you leave behind? And
what can ease the makin' of that journey? Why, the sharin of it,

working side by side, sharin' the joys and the sorrows, the new stories that you will share around the campfire time and time again. The jokin', singin', learnin' new songs, makin' new songs together. We're paddling in the same canoe! We gotta pull together. All for one and one for all. That's what makes the journey easier.

RUBY
THESE LANDS

RUBY:

(*taking off hat*) Many paths lead me through the meadows, the forests, the deserts, the mountains. The rolling hills of grain lying in neat rows up and down the fields, around the knolls; some gray with too much rain, spoiled, useless for anything but straw... some golden in the sun. I feel a stinging rise in my nose and throat, why? I see these fields all cut, the swathes winding over the hillocks, and I imagine running, no, riding across, no fences on these huge tracts of land. Riding like the wind. These lands. Full of all us creatures breathing and feeding and growing and crawling and walking and swimming and flying and running and scampering and singing and calling and wailing and bellowing and chirping and chattering and splashing and running and rearing and flying and flitting and floating and sailing and swimming and running and riding and eating and laughing and crying and loving and jigging and reeling!

MUSIC: Reeling i.e. Smash the Window

Encore.

MUSIC: Halfbreed

Ruby sings Halfbreed with Band

END OF PLAY

MARIE CLEMENTS has been active as a performer and playwright in theatres across Canada and the United States. Marie's plays have attracted attention nationally and internationally, and have been produced at such venues as LA's Mark Taper Forum, Minneapolis's Playwrights Centre, the International Festival of Native Playwrights in LA, Illinois and New York, the New Literature Festival in Germany, the Women, Text and Technologies Festival in Leeds, England, the Boomerang Festival, in Pont-a Mousson, France and Montreal's prestigious Festival des Ameriques. Over the past two years she has been a writer in residence at various centres including, the National Theatre School, Playwrights Workshop in Montreal, The Firehall Arts Centre, Rumble Theatre and the Banff Playwrights Colony. Her past works include award-winning *Now look what you made me do*, *The Girl who Swam Forever*, *Urban Tattoo*, *The Unnatural and Accidental Women* and numerous other collectives and collaborations. Marie is currently working on her script *Burning Vision*, a commission by Rumble Theatre in Vancouver, to be produced April 2002, and the commissioned script Copper Thunderbird with Les Onidinnok Theatre in Montreal.

MARGO KANE (Cree/Saulteaux) is an interdisciplinary artist who has taken an active role in encouraging and initiating many creative projects in First Nations communities, as well as non-Native communities, that seek to develop cross-cultural understanding through the arts. Over the past twenty-five years, she has been recognized as a storyteller, dancer, singer, animator, video and installation artist, director, producer, writer and teacher. Her original one-woman production, *Moonlodge*, has been acclaimed across Canada, and toured to New York City, Ireland and The Festival of the Dreaming, Sydney, the Melbourne Fringe and Brisbane's Dar Festival in Australia. *The River – Home* is her video installation and performance developed with an ensemble that she trained on forming Full Circle: First Nations Performance in Vancouver where she currently resides. Full Circle is her company formed to initiate and explore the development of contemporary work that is rooted in

First Peoples experience. The Talking Stick Festival produced with that company will enter it's second year to coincide with National Aboriginal Day. Presently, she is planning to produce and tour *Confessions of an Indian Cowboy* later this year.

GREG DANIELS is a multi-disciplinary author who is based out of Regina. His list of production credits include: *Blind Girl Last Night* in 1992, *Percy's Edge* in 1995 and *Four Horses* in 1998, all produced at 25th Street Theatre in Saskatoon. He has also written *Night Driving*, a radio play produced by CBC, and served as a Board member for Sakewewak Artist Collective and Neutral Ground Artist Run Centre, and as Council member for Circle Vision Artist Corporation. He is currently completing his first poetry manuscript entitled *And Steam Rose from the Ground Early that Morning*.